Through Peter's Eyes

by Hazel Morgan

Through Peter's Eyes

by
Hazel Morgan

with a Preface by Professor Stanley Hauerwas
and a Foreword by Professor Stephen Sykes

Arthur James
BOOK PUBLISHERS

First published in 1990
by Arthur James Limited
One, Cranbourne Road, London N10 2BT, England

British Library Cataloguing in Publication Data

Morgan, Hazel
Through Peter's eyes
1. Down's syndrome children
I. Title
362.3

ISBN 0-85305-305-7

Typeset in London by Christel Ivo

Printed by Martin's of Berwick

Dedication

I dedicate this book to my father,
who called Peter 'Pedro'

Contents

PREFACE
by Professor Stanley Hauerwas
The Divinity School, Duke University,
Durham, North Carolina, USA

Christopher Nolan's *Under the Eye of the Clock* (St Martin's Press, New York, 1987 and Weidenfeld & Nicolson Ltd., London, 1987; Pan Books Ltd., London, 1988) stands alone for giving voice to the disabled. It does so, of course, because it is the voice of the body and speech crippled, but mind-enlivened young man who is able to make language dance so that we can enter his extraordinay world of helplessness and strength. His book is unique but Hazel Morgan in *Through Peter's Eyes* is engaged in the same moral task. She is trying to give voice to the voiceless by helping us to see that Peter Morgan is, like us, vulnerable and thus capable of friendship.

When a mentally handicapped child is born, our most cherished illusions about life are challenged. As parents we often learn that we subject our children to our own fantasies about success and what it means to be normal. We learn that we do not live in a society that genuinely wants to protect and enhance the life of the vulnerable. We learn too that our friends turn away from us, pained by their inability "to do anything". We learn that we must fight the very bureaucracies put in place to help, as they simply cannot see that Peter has particular needs, as Peter. Most of all, we confront the attitude that it would be better if such children did not exist — the attitude that often appears as compassion but actually denies their existence.

Mrs Morgan, however, will not let us still Peter's voice. She has been schooled by Peter's cries, educated by his needs. She has learned to rejoice in his joys. By being so formed she has, like Christopher Nolan, given us the means to understand Peter's world a little better—to understand that Peter rejoices in a plastic pool of water, that Peter loves the sounds of birds, that Peter is enthralled by Christmas decorations, that Peter is confused and upset by unfamiliar surroundings. We then begin to realise that Peter is not a subject for our compassion, but an essential part of our community. We do not have Peters because they may make us better parents, societies, or people, but we discover that we are more than we knew because Peters are more than we thought.

We are therefore in Mrs Morgan's debt for helping us hear with Peter, feel with Peter, smell with Peter, cry with Peter, laugh with Peter and, most of all, love as Peter loves. There is of course much agony in this book: there is weariness, there is despair, there is anger. We would not trust Mrs Morgan's account if she were not honest about her frustrations over Peter, and with the world that denies his existence. Yet the remarkable moral witness Mrs Morgan makes is that her suffering with and on Peter's behalf is wonderfully bounded by Peter's voice.

We must recognise however that we live in societies that may soon wish to still the voice of Peter. Listen to the speech by Christopher Nolan, read by his mother, as he received a 'People of the Year' award:

> He glanced often at his mother. There she stood conveying his words for him. She it was who gambled with her sensibilities and got from his signals the gist of his thoughts. Now she stood at the podium holding his typewritten words in her hand and read: 'A brain damaged baby cannot ponder why a mother cannot communicate with it, and unless it gains

parental love and stimulation it stymies, and thus retardation fulsomely establishes its soul-destroying seabed." Conscious of the breathtaking sacrifice involved in what his family did for him, yet he detected where destiny beckoned. The future for babies like him never looked more promising, but now society frowned upon giving spastic babies a right to life. Now they threatened to abort babies like him, to detect in advance their handicapped state, to burrow through the womb and label them for death, to baffle their mothers with fear for their coming, and yet the spastic baby would ever be the soul which would never kill, maim, breed falsehood or hate brotherhood. Why then does society fear the crippled child, and why does it hail the able-bodied child and crow over what may in time become a potential executioner?

(page 119, page 156 in the Pan edition)

If we have an alternative it will be because we have learned to listen to the voice of a Peter.

FOREWORD
by Professor Stephen Sykes
Regius Professor of Divinity, University of Cambridge

I was born in 1939. It is, therefore, within my life-time that a European government has sanctioned the large scale killing of the mentally handicapped and disordered, a policy which was carried out by doctors and nurses, the healing professions. The approximately 200,000 persons who perished were murdered because they were too expensive to maintain during time of war, and because it was thought that better use could be made of the hospital accommodation which they occupied. Some parents agreed with the programme; others, kept in ignorance, were simply told of their relative's death. In the end the killing was stopped partly because of public protests from church leaders, though it has to be said that there was also some collusion from Christian institutions and individuals.

None of this can be written off as a German aberration. It is our civilisation, in our century, responding to pressures we can recognise out of moral resources no different from our own. We forget it at our peril. And if you, the reader of this book, and I, the writer of the foreword to it, consider that the medicalised killing of even one Down's Syndrome child would be an absolutely intolerable outrage against humanity, we had better know why. We have no grounds for simply trusting the ethical instincts of the late twentieth-century Europeans, not even of medical experts.

It will not, however, do simply to say that killing people is wrong. What is at issue is, in the end of the day, not merely the right of a human being to life, and the fact that by 'human being' is meant any human birth. As Hazel Morgan's story makes clear, attitudes towards 'the handicapped' contribute to the progressive erosion of the idea of their right to life to the point where their being is defined as 'not worth saving' (*Ballastexistenzen* was the poisonous concept invented by the Nazi ideologists). If we are to challenge this more insidious trend clearly present in our own society, we shall have to have an ethic which embraces the handicapped, and welcomes and affirms their personhood.

But who, in that last sentence, is 'we'? Hazel Morgan writes out of clear Christian conviction and important aspects of her narrative are rooted in the support she received from the Christian community. Every carer for a handicapped, chronically sick or bed-ridden person knows how essential it is to be able to share the burdens with others. But what others? Fortunately British society has a long tradition of organisations which provide support for carers and a lobby for the needs of the sufferers. But no voluntary society can come anywhere close to the Christian churches in their coverage of and responsibility for every household in the country, and their moral resources for caring and for sharing the burdens of care. The question is this: are they sufficiently persuaded that alertness to these needs is an integral part of Christian ministry?

As a Christian priest and theologian, I want to underline the importance of certain features of Hazel Morgan's account which I see as profoundly consistent with the resources of Christian ethics. She, her husband and their elder son *live with* Peter: she sustains and contends for his *dignity* and *worth:* her relationship with him is reciprocal to the point where, though he is speechless, she *converses with him,* graciously endowing his inarticulacy with intelligibility: she understands his self-worth as enhanced by *hospitality,* for which prepares him. All this time she speaks to me of a God whose very being is with us, who accords us dignity and worth as created in His image and likeness, who converses with us, endowing our inarticulacy with understanding, and for whom fellowship at table is a chosen symbol of acceptance and love. Members of Christian communities have every reason to read this book as a challenge and encouragement to the reality of their faith; but still more to the quality of their lives *as communities.*

Professor Stanley Hauerwas, the Christian ethicist from Duke Divinity School in the USA who has thought deeply about these matters, puts the issue thus:

> The true moral question is what kind of community ought we to be so that we can welcome and care for the other in our midst without that 'otherness' being used to justify discrimination.*

It cuts no ice for Christians to urge society at large to adopt this or that policy towards the handicapped, if their own practices as church communities do not reflect their beliefs. We shall have the right to proclaim an ethic which embraces the handicapped and welcomes and affirms their personhood if, and only if, we welcome and affirm them.

And I know of no better personal concept of the challenge of the 'other' to our corporate lives, and the enrichment to be experienced in meeting it, than the modest and compelling book you are about to read.

* *The Moral Challenge of the Handicapped*
  by Stanley Hauerwas, 'Suffering Presence', University of Notre Dame Press 1986, p 185

INTRODUCTION

'A shattering experience.'
'Your world must have stood still for a time.'
'It's something everyone must always fear.'

These were some of the remarks made at the time of Peter's birth, in 1977. Peter, our son, has Down's Syndrome. Although this was a totally unexpected occurrence and one which has caused us to face many problems, it has greatly enriched our lives too. I hope the following pages will demonstrate that very clearly.

In the months immediately after Peter's birth we received considerable help. We also gained great pleasure from his presence in the family. We thought ourselves fortunate that he was born at a time when services for families with a handicapped child were improving. No longer were parents expected, as a matter of course, to put their handicapped offspring into an institution. Since 1971, every child has had the right to education and so we did not have to face the possibility that our son might be judged ineducable, as could have happened previously. The outlook seemed brighter for handicapped children and their families.

We became aware, after some time, however, that we had been too optimistic, that services are often limited and that there were, and are, subtle threats to the rights of handicapped people in our society. When the question of Peter's heart surgery arose I learnt that, at that time at least, the retarded could not be sure of receiving the same treatment as normal people. The shock I felt over this was intensified several years later when the 'Baby Alexandra' and 'Dr Arthur' cases became news, and we realised that handicapped babies could be very vulnerable from the moment of their birth.

In August 1981 Alexandra, a baby with Down's Syndrome, was made a ward of court in order that she might have a life-saving operation to unblock her intestine, as her parents had refused to give their consent. Sections of the media emphasised the problems caused for parents by these children, rather than the children's delightful characters. A vigorous debate followed in the columns of newspapers, and in the media generally, about the rights and wrongs of allowing a handicapped baby to die when appropriate medical treatment was available.

This question was discussed with even greater intensity following the trial of Dr Arthur in October of that year. He was alleged to have 'allowed baby John Pearson to die', following rejection by his parents, by prescribing only nursing care and a pain-killing drug. The rights of parents and of their handicapped babies, and the role of doctors, were debated with fierce emotion. Professionals, parents of handicapped children, churchmen and the public in general joined in, displaying a variety of attitudes and prejudices. There was considerable sympathy for the doctor, who was clearly a caring man, and many felt that this was a decision for parents to make in the light of medical advice. Yet could the parents—at such a vulnerable time, when they had just learned of their child's condition —make the best decision, or might they make one which they would later regret?

I myself felt that the right to life of the handicapped child was paramount, and I was shocked that the issue was even being debated in a civilised society! How could other arguments supercede what was to me the fundamental one? The situation seemed paradoxical. On one hand, much was being done to improve the quality of life for the disabled through better services and through policies of integration and community care. On the other hand, their very right to exist was being questioned. How could society be so ambivalent?

I was worried about some of the ignorance that was being shown about Down's Syndrome. It is a condition which brings varying degrees of retardation. One correspondent on a national newspaper wrote as if all such children were cabbages, whereas they are characters. Much of the debate centred on the question of 'the quality of life', as if there were a certain level of existence below which life becomes unbearable. Since the discussion concerned two Down's Syndrome babies it seemed that, in the minds of some people, the enjoyment of simple pleasures did not constitute a satisfactory life. Most children with Down's Syndrome and adults can be content in the right environment. To redress the balance, it was lovely to read a letter from a parent telling of his Down's son's pleasure in sport, his warmth and his caring attitude, displayed towards others more handicapped than himself at his boarding school.

As a Christian I wanted the church to speak out on this issue as I felt that the care of the vulnerable and the needy was at the heart of the Gospel. Cardinal Hume and the Chief Rabbi strongly upheld the rights of the handicapped. I learnt, however, that the Anglican Church believed that there could be no blanket statement. It was a complex issue that required consideration by their Board of Social Responsibility. There were grey areas, it was said, whereas I saw it in black and white. Any grey area was very narrow indeed. In the case of a very profoundly handicapped baby who, in order to survive would need multiple and painful surgery, there might be a case for caring for and feeding the baby, but withholding surgical treatment, but never a case for starvation or the refusal of routine operations. This too is a fine and difficult balance. It is one which is recognised by the Catholic Church. The two cases under discussion concerned Down's babies whose capacity to enjoy life was potentially similar to, or even greater, than Peter's. How could there be a debate on such an issue?

Perhaps even more shattering to me was the fact that the same discussion was going on among our friends, and similar divisions arose. People whom we liked and trusted sided with Dr Arthur. One member of my church told me that all Dr Arthur was doing was sending the child to heaven sooner! I now realised that people around us might view Peter's life on a level different from that of their own children.

I remember, on another occasion, discussing with a close friend the allocation of limited medical resources and she posed for me the dilemma of choosing between treatment for Philip, our elder son, and Peter, assuming that I valued the boys differently.

I felt overwhelmed by these revelations. Each morning I would wake up thinking that, in the eyes of some in our society, Peter and those like him are *less* valuable than their 'normal' counterparts. The unfairness and the dangers in this attitude gnawed away at me. How could I come to terms with such thinking? What could I do about it? In the end I had to recognise that this problem did indeed exist within our society and that, sad as I was about it, to become thoroughly miserable did no good. I must rather work for the development of a positive view of the handicapped.

Shortly after that I received an unexpected telephone call from an adoption agency which was moving into the field of the 'hard to place' child, asking me if I would serve on their panel. This seemed to provide an opening. The solution to parental rejection is to find a loving home for the child, rather than ending his or her life.

Some years later (as it is now), this book is a further attempt to uphold the rights of the handicapped child to enjoy life. It will show his or her capacity for happiness. His or her pleasures may be simpler than ours, but they are no less real. Parts of the book are written through Peter's eyes. This does have its difficulties as, inevitably, I have endowed him with greater understanding and awareness than he actually has, particularly in his early days. I am using words (as I have to do) which are a tool he has not learned to handle. I hope, however, that I have gone some way to conveying what he may have felt at particular times, and I have especially tried to show what gives him happiness.

I would be less than honest if I depicted the life of a handicapped child and his family as a 'bed of roses', by describing the blooms and neglecting the thorns. I have therefore tried to show the problems we have encountered. Each family will have its own particular difficulties and its own individual situation, depending on the nature and degree of the handicap, but many of these difficulties will be experienced, to a greater or lesser degree, by others. I hope this will help to further the understanding of the needs of handicapped people and their families, and will also increase awareness that some problems (such as the isolation of the handicapped person) are the result of public attitudes and the way we organise services within our society. *They are not the result of the handicap itself, but of our reactions to it.*

I have tried, too, to relate Peter's condition and that of

19

those like him to my own Christian faith because I believe that the Gospel should illuminate this area and provide some answer to the way we care for handicapped people in our community.

Note: The terms 'mongol' and 'mongolism', which were usual at the time Peter was born, are now discouraged and the term 'Down's Syndrome' substituted for them. The latter is therefore used in this book wherever a child with this handicap is described.

Chapter 1

ARE THEY PLEASED WITH ME?

I am in her arms. She holds me close. She says 'little Peter'. I snuggle to her, but not for long. A soft sheet is wrapped around me. I lie alone. Where is she, the one who said 'little Peter'? There are pains inside me. I cry. I am picked up and something soft is pushed inside my mouth. My tongue moves against it, up and down. Now there is a stabbing inside my nose. This stops and my tummy feels warm. I am content at last. I sleep. Again those pains, again I suck a little, again liquid slides into me and I am happy.

She is here. It seems a long time since I saw her. She cuddles me, but soon I am back in my cot. Sleeping, waking, feeding, sleeping, waking, feeding. She comes and holds me. I sleep again.

New people with deep voices are beside me. They sound grave. They undress me and put something hard and cold on my chest. Aren't they pleased with me? They prick me. I cry.

Another man visits me with the lady they call mummy. He cuddles me and talks to me. I am beginning to suck better; my nose no longer feels blocked. I am glad. I think they are pleased.

There is a reassuring noise around me. Other babies cry. The nurses call me 'Peter'. They say I am sweet.

Mummy comes. She feels different. Her clothes are rough against my cheek. Is she going away? The door closes behind her. I feel sad. I feel ill. I gasp for breath. I feel pain in my chest. I am afraid . . .

The pain goes away; I sleep.

Mummy is here again. She cuddles me. She gives me a bottle. The nurses ask her if everything is all right at home. What is home? How is her little boy? Who is her little boy?

They both come today. Mummy feeds me, then they seem to hold me especially tightly as if to reassure me. They look sad. Aren't they pleased with me, any more? 'You'll come home soon', they say. 'You will meet Philip.' Perhaps I don't need to have this awful sinking feeling inside.

Peter was born at about 1 am on Tuesday, January 11, by normal delivery. Hardly had he been placed in my arms before he was taken away to be warmed under a special lamp and then to be nursed in the Special Care Nursery. It all happened with a quiet acceptance on my part, as if it was almost to be expected.

I had not anticipated problems at the end of my pregnancy, and yet, on the arrival of my second son, I felt none of the overwhelming emotions of excited anticipation and intense relief and joy that I had experienced at the birth of my first child. It was as if I already knew that the tiny baby, who had lodged temporarily in my arms and then been whisked away, was bringing a very special responsibility.

For the first ten days I stayed in the hospital in the ward for mothers with babies who had been delivered by forceps or caesarean section. I was the only one without a cot at her side, and the only one who could move with any kind of ease! I would walk the long corridor to the special care nursery at intervals throughout the day to visit Peter, initially being allowed to hold him and then, as he changed from tube to bottle feeding, to feed and

22

change him. I was cocooned in the hospital routine, enjoyed the friendship of the mums and appreciated their enquiries about Peter.

As I look back, I must have been in something of a daze not to have realised the gravity of the situation sooner. I first assumed that he had some physical problem that could be rectified. I was told that he had the signs of a post mature baby, although I believed him to be ten days early, that his blood sugar levels were wrong, that he went blue. After several days, I received a visit from the consultant paediatrician, who took a blood sample from me and told me he was concerned about the baby. A nurse said that he was very sweet really. What did this mean?

My husband Andy visited regularly and he too was initially hoping for improvements. On the first Sunday, my mother brought in my two-year-old son to see me. He was excited to be there and wanted to look at his brother. With his granny, he was allowed to peer through the special care window.

On the second Thursday of Peter's life, I went home. I would come into the hospital to feed him, but I could also give some time to Philip who felt himself very neglected by his mum.

On the following Friday, my husband and I were due to see the consultant about the results of the blood tests. By this time, I think that I had realised the seriousness of the situation. When my own General Practitioner visited me on my first day out of hospital, I asked whether blood tests were required to diagnose Down's Syndrome, not that I thought Peter had the features associated with that condition.

When the consultant told us that he had bad news for us, that our son was a 'mongol', it did not come as a surprise. He gave us a detailed explanation of the chromosomal abnormality, which occurs at conception and assured us that it was not, in any way, our fault. In the common form that Peter had (Trisomy 21), it was seen as a chance occurrence, for which scientists had yet to establish a cause. There was a link with ageing but at thirty-two, I was not in the high-risk category. He then made a strange statement to the effect that when we got over the 'shame and guilt', we would find that we had a loving child. I found it very odd that we had been given a scientific explanation of the handicap, for which we were not seen as responsible and then it had been suggested we might feel guilt! Subsequently, I learnt that guilt was considered to be a strong emotion at the birth of a handicapped child, but I believe this to have been exaggerated.

We did not feel resentful either. We rather had a feeling of acceptance of this tiny baby, who nestled against us as we held him. He had been very poorly in the first week of his life and particularly on the day that I went home. This had made him all the more precious to us and we desperately wanted him to survive. Philip must have a brother close in age, I kept thinking, although I now look back on this with wry amusement as mentally their ages are at least twelve years apart. Nonetheless they have a close bond between them, having grown up together.

After being given a few moments to collect ourselves, one of the nurses came in to offer us a cup of tea. I casually asked whether I would be able to feed Peter. 'Oh! you are not going to reject him then?', she said. I was surprised and replied roundly 'of course not.' I was being introduced into a world in which dark words like shame, guilt, resentment, rejection seemed to be common currency. We loved this tiny boy and could only do our best for him and his brother.

As Andy and I talked over this unexpected occurrence in our lives that weekend, it seemed as if I had a heightened awareness about a group of people to whom I had given very little thought in the past, the mentally handicapped. If I felt guilt in any sense, it was guilt that I had given so little consideration to these vulnerable members of our society and I wanted to find out all I could about their lives and needs. The hospital gave me the address of the Down's Babies Association (now called The Down's Syndrome Association) and so I learnt that to say 'mongol' was out of date! I also wrote to Mencap. Andy felt great sadness for Peter in that he would not be able to develop normally, but I had a very strong conviction that he could be happy, indeed possibly happier than normal folk with their complex thoughts, if he lived in the right environment. This carried me through. One fact which helped me to have that attitude was the story of Norman that my grandmother told me as a child. He was a man with Down's Syndrome whom she visited weekly to help with painting, basketwork and piano-playing. He was the son of the vicar at the church where she was organist. He had been responsible for pumping the instrument and sometimes the music would cease in the middle of a hymn! I had met Norman on a couple of occasions and he clearly had many endearing qualities and so I had in my mind the picture of a delightful handicapped man living with his family to set alongside the stereotypes of the institutionalised mentally handicapped that I would sometimes see going for walks on a Sunday afternoon.

Four months previously I had regained my Christian faith. That helped me to be able to pray about Peter; nonetheless, it forced me to face again the question of why God allows suffering in the world. On one hand, I could not believe God wanted children to be born impaired, and yet I believed Peter and those like him were somehow 'special' and that good would come from their lives. It is not a full explanation of course, but I believe it is important to see God's presence in the suffering in the world and in the love that is thereby generated. Peter was going to create a lot of love in his life and already we could see this in the care he was receiving in the hospital.

Peter spent three weeks in Special Care; he developed a severe rash before he was able to come home. We had been very fortunate in the treatment that he and we received. I later heard stories of parents learning of their child's condition in very unsympathetic ways: a mother being told by a complete stranger without her husband present at 6am having gone to sleep the previous night believing that all was well with the new baby. I believe parents should learn the truth in the early days, that they should be told together, by a senior doctor, and promised more information when they have had time to assimilate the news that their child is mentally handicapped.

Chapter 2

I LOOK UP AT THE BEAMS

I awake, it is all different. I look up. There are dark lines against the whiteness. My mummy and daddy seem pleased. They look at me, they smile. There is someone much smaller. He smiles brightly. 'Can I hold Peter?' he says. 'Can I touch him, will he play with me?' What is 'play'? They pick me up. 'Sit down, Philip. Take care! Here is your brother.' I am lowered on to a knee. It does not feel so safe, his arms are small, but he holds tight. He has bright eyes and a large smile. I like him, the one they call my 'brother'. Am I playing?

The pains come in my tummy. I cry. 'He does not like me' says Philip. I want to tell him it isn't true; it's the pains in my tummy. Mummy says 'It's all right, Philip, he's hungry.' 'Can *I* feed him?' asks Philip. 'Another time' replies my mummy and I am in her arms. I suck, the warmth invades me. I am content, I am at peace.

From now on I wake in a room alone. Through the side of my cot, I see pattern and colour, blues and yellows. There is only one dark beam on this ceiling to examine. When the pain comes, I cry and Mummy feeds me and changes me. She lifts me and carries me downstairs. I like the jerky movement.

I look at many beams, the lines please me. The shrill tones of my brother entertain me. 'What are we going to do today, Mummy? Will you play with me? Can I get my cars out?' Questions, questions and more questions. 'We must go for a walk' says Mummy. I am dressed up, put in my pram. We go out of the door with a jolt. A blast of cold air hits me each time we leave the house. I like the up and down motion of the pram. I can look up and see brown patterns, with light dancing through, sometimes brightly, sometimes giving them a greyish hue. There are many sounds; a soft roar, the light rustling of leaves . . . Philip says 'Can we go on the river banks?' My pram bumps up and down. It feels funny. Suddenly there is a loud peal of bells. There is a lot of noise but it excites me. Then there is only the sound of rushing water and the wind in the trees . . .

Once Peter was home, we felt more vulnerable. Hospital had provided good support and had shouldered the responsibility. The prime care of a tiny baby was now, however, in our own hands. He was slow to feed and had to be winded three or four times when taking a bottle, as is

27

often the case with a Down's Syndrome child. We were fortunate that we lived in a friendly neighbourhood round the corner from the boarding-school where Andy taught. Very frequently, when friends first knew about Peter's condition, their first remark was 'I am so sorry'. I wanted to say 'Don't be sorry. Peter is alive and we are happy to have him.' In fact I would murmur, 'It's all right', lest they should think me odd and knowing I would probably have said the same thing in their shoes! Many friends offered practical assistance like shopping for us or inviting Philip to play. Gifts were showered on us. Some showed great sensitivity and told me how beautiful Peter was; I wholeheartedly agreed with them, though photos reveal he was a funny little scrap as small babies often are. One or two avoided mentioning him altogether which I found hard, although I later realised that it was more from embarrassment than anything else. Letters poured in which told us stories of Down's people and we found those most helpful. In one case, some friends wrote very movingly of what they had learnt from the death of their brain-damaged baby at six weeks of age. Peter was in a sense opening new doors in our lives, in that people would sometimes speak very freely with us because we had experienced the birth of a handicapped child.

At first I felt incapable of living beyond the present, as if the enormity of the problems of Peter's future could not be faced. Gradually, we began to look forward and we experienced our own outlook being challenged and changed, our assumptions being undermined. We recognised that Peter would be living a life that was in many ways the antithesis of that which is regarded as desirable in our own society. He would not earn great sums of money. He would be unlikely to marry or even live independently. Academic achievement would not be his. Yet given the right circumstances, he could be happy and enjoy simple pleasures no less real than they would be for anyone else. He had something to teach us.

I shed very few tears at the time of Peter's birth, but one morning at breakfast I did weep. In the post, we had received our first set of literature from Mencap, and on the front of one pamphlet was a picture of a group of mentally handicapped people working together with not a normal person in sight. Was this Peter's future—a world away from ordinary life? It was hard to take. Later I would learn how barriers are being broken down as the report *Care in the Community* was being accepted as government policy following the Jay report of 1975, but nonetheless there are still real problems. My fears of Peter's segregation were by no means groundless.

We thus gradually came to terms with our new situation, valuing our friends and family (the two grannies stayed in turn in the early weeks), learning to receive help at a time when we could do nothing else, because the task of bringing up a handicapped child and a lively boy approaching three were enormous, and rapidly finding out about mental handicap, as we read as much as we could.

I lie back in my bouncing chair. My feet touch the ground. I rock myself up and down. I like that. I can see more. My brother is running around on his chunky legs, talking, busy with his many activities. Often I sleep and just hear the soft hum of voices.

Mummy takes me out of the car and pushes me into a building with plain walls. We go into a room and the lady there puts me on a mat and pushes my feet one at a time. I bend my knee again

29

and again. Isn't she ever going to stop. Why does she do it? At last some rest, some lovely sounds start near my head, I try to turn, a hand is placed behind my shoulder, I begin to move towards the music. 'Good boy' they say. Why good boy? I flop on my tummy, the music throbs inside me, I like it, it makes me feel peaceful. I fall asleep . . .

Now when I bump down the step of our front door, I am propped up. It is much more interesting. We go around the corner, there is greenness everywhere. Boys are running around on it. My brother is more interested in his little bat and ball, my daddy plays with him . . . Today there was a new sound on our walk. My brother is scuffling through brown, yellow and orange leaves. He kicks them in the air.

They sit me on the floor, but this time they remove the soft cushions from behind me. I am still, and then lurch back into their waiting hands. They sit me up again. This time many minutes pass before I topple over.

Although our ideas were changing, most of my thoughts were on the daily routine: meals, feeds, washing, shopping, play, walks. February and March are often grey months in the year and I appreciated the friends who continued to call or offer help, especially those who gave us lifts to hospital as we did not have a car, although we soon realised we must purchase one.

There were many appointments and contacts with professionals in those early months. The midwife came initially then she handed over to the health visitor who was already a friend from Philip's babyhood.

Our GP gave us a clear exposition of Down's Syndrome. After a couple of visits to the paediatrician, the overall care of Peter's development was handed over to the consultant psychiatrist at the local mental handicap hospital. Peter was able to attend a regular clinic there so that the occupational therapist could help him along with other Down's children. He was referred to a paediatric cardiologist in Newcastle and the likelihood of a hole in the heart established. The educational psychologist came after about five months to review his progress and was pleased. The community medical officer made contact. During some weeks we were inundated with visits and visitors. I was very impressed with the treatment we received, as if everyone was trying to do their best for Peter. Nonetheless, it was a tiring business.

We received training schedules from the Down's Syndrome Association and, with advice from the occupational therapist, would put Peter through his paces, encouraging him to turn over, to reach out or do whatever was appropriate to his stage of development. I subsequently came to regard these training programmes with some ambivalence. They were helpful in that I felt that I could assist Peter's progress, but they could inspire some guilt feelings if I put off doing them; sometimes I think they can be an obstacle to enjoying the baby for himself. They are useful therefore only as long as they can be kept in the right perspective. A handicapped baby has, after all, the same needs as a normal baby for love, food, sleep and stimulation. Hospital appointments and visits from professionals served to remind us that our situation was *not* normal, but by and large, we tried to be an ordinary family with two small boys. I came to realise that, in many ways, our task was easier than that of parents whose *first* child was handicapped, for they do not necessarily have knowledge of what a normal baby would do and no other child to distract them from their worries. On the other hand, if they have more children, they have the advantage of being able to bring up the children similarly for a while. In our case Philip mentally was growing away from Peter; there was never a stage when they could play as equals.

As Peter became more aware, he would sit in his bouncing chair with his feet on the ground moving himself up and down while watching Philip and his friends playing. At five months he began to smile and seem more sociable. In the autumn he began to sit up and his drum became his favourite toy. Sometimes he would chuckle for the sheer joy of being alive as he sat in a pool of sunlight, making us all feel happier. The Easter and summer holidays gave us a chance to relax as a family, either visiting my parents in North Yorkshire or being at home. The future was beginning to look much more hopeful.

Chapter 3

I CAN'T SIT UP ANY MORE

I like looking round this room. We don't come in here very often. The chairs have blue, green, brown leafy patterns. In the corner pictures move. It makes me happy. I bang my drum. A sudden jerkiness seizes me, my body twitches, I can't stop it. I keel over. I'm frightened. I cry . . .

A kindly gentleman takes me in his arms. He has glasses like my daddy. His hands are firm, his voice confident. 'May the Lord Jesus heal you, Peter.' What does that mean? I feel warm inside. I feel at peace . . .

I am once more surrounded by nurses and gentlemen in white coats. They keep looking at me. I examine the white ceiling. Only the bluebird hanging on my cot, playing my favourite tune makes me happy. They give me a sweet liquid on a spoon after meals. I feel sleepy.

It seems a long time since it was so warm in the garden. Mummy has filled a plastic pool with water. Philip runs in and out, splashing. Mummy takes off my clothes and puts me in the water. It feels good, the warmth around me, the sun beating down on me. She supports me behind my shoulders. Why can't I sit up like I used to . . . ?

Today I sat up again! I was able to reach for my drum on my own! I feel alert, awake. The greenness is so bright, the light dances on the leaves. I laugh. Why do I feel so different? Mummy hasn't been saying 'take your medicine like a good boy' . . .

In the November of 1977, Peter began to twitch. At first, I thought nothing of it. However, when those twitches became more pronounced so that the whole upper part of his body would jerk, clearly something worrying was happening. I told the staff at Earl's House, the subnormality hospital, and Peter was given Epilim to prevent him having a fit. We were then sent to the children's hospital in Newcastle to have an electro encephalogram. It turned out that the pattern was not normal and that there was an indication that he was having hypsarhythmic attacks. Our own GP had known a girl in his practice with this same unusual condition, and he gave us a gloomy picture. There was the threat of further mental retardation hanging over Peter. I made an appointment with the consultant psychiatrist and, although her prognosis was not quite so harsh, she kept saying "I'm so sorry, he was doing so well". Peter would be sent for a further EEG to see if the pattern became clearer.

33

I was in the doldrums. It seemed to matter tremendously that Peter might suffer further mental retardation. While there was progress we could be optimistic. Now I felt shut in on myself, as if I were in a long dark tunnel. I was unable to communicate my fears to my friends, hoping these fears would prove to be unfounded. My faith was also at a low ebb. I prayed for Peter, but without great conviction. God seemed far away. I waited each day for Peter to have these salaam attacks. They occurred once or twice and lasted five or ten minutes. Peter was no longer able to sit himself up.

Help came unexpectedly. I had been attending the local Anglican church, and one Sunday the rector said that he and his wife had the conviction that Peter needed prayer. 'He does' I said and proceeded to tell him about my fears and worries over Peter's new condition. He asked if he could come to talk to us about prayer for healing one evening. We then learnt that a healing ministry was nothing new in the church but there was a growing emphasis on it in the renewal movement. He said that, if we agreed, he would pray regularly with Peter, laying on hands. Andy, who at this stage could not accept all Christian doctrine, nevertheless assented readily, and indeed with greater faith than I had. We all began to pray for Peter's recovery.

About four months after the first attacks, Peter was sent for another EEC and this showed up clearly the hypsarhythmic pattern. He was rushed into hospital to be observed while being treated with mogadon and steroids. This coincided with a Parish weekend away on the theme of wholeness. We later heard that, on the Saturday evening, a lot of time was spent praying for Peter. From the time he went into hospital, he never had another attack, although the medication had not had a chance to work. He stayed in hospital for a week and then went for another EEG. This showed a normal pattern.

Peter was kept on steroids for a month and mogadon for

a further two. Apparently children's tolerance of mogadon is much higher than that of an adult and surprisingly he was not asleep all day. He was, nonetheless, very 'floppy' and it was not until he was taken off all medication in the July of 1978 and he began to sit up again and be alert, that the fact that he was really healed could sink in properly.

We do not know what effect these attacks had on his long term development. He certainly made rapid progress in the first few months after his recovery as if he was trying to make up for lost time, but gradually the pace slackened and he emerged as a slow Down's boy, whereas in his babyhood he had seemed comparatively advanced.

This experience taught us a great deal. It gave us insight into the anguish of parents and their children when they suffer from fits or regressive illness; we were fortunate that, once again, we could look forward. We learnt more about the power of prayer and, after further reading and discussion, Andy sought Confirmation.

Chapter 4

I'M LEARNING QUICKLY

My brother is beside me. Boxes, bags are piled up round us. Why don't we start? I cry, I want to go, I want to feel the car move, the purr of the engine. At last it throbs to life. I stop crying. I watch our house disappear, houses flash by. Other cars come towards us, blues, greens, reds; there's a whoosh as they pass. I am filled with excitement. Now it is green as I look out of the window, my eyelids are heavy, they flicker . . . As I open my eyes, we are still driving. The hills are purple and green. I've never seen anything like it before. At last we stop. I am carried into a house with white walls, there are lots of pictures, I have been here before. 'Hello, Peter, it's Nana'. 'Hello, Pedro.' I am put on Papa's knee. I like it, it's bigger than anyone else's. My papa has an enormous face. The glasses are bigger than Daddy's. He smiles. 'Well, Pedro'. Why does he call me Pedro? I laugh. I want to tell him I like him. I make my happy popping sounds.

I'm high up in the air, taller than my daddy. I peep over his shoulder. The movement is jerky and uneven as we tramp over the moors. I wish I could see Daddy's face. I look at the back of his head. I look down at Philip, with his big coloured ball under his arm.

They put me down. The ground is warm, not hard yet not soft, it is yellow brown. I put out my hand to touch it. It seems to move. I try to pick it up. I take a handful, it runs through my fingers and falls silently back on the ground. I grab more, I put it to my mouth and lick it. It is gritty and crunchy, I like it . . .

The second part of 1978 was, on the whole, a much smoother time. We were encouraged by Peter's progress. During the long summer holidays, we spent a fortnight in the Lake District, renting part of the house of a lovely Cumbrian couple. They made us very welcome and the wife would often leave out chocolate for the boys to find when we came back from our outings. Although Philip's legs were still too short to go on a really long walk, one day we did manage five miles. Peter would sit up high on Andy's shoulders in a back pack, enjoying the movement and the view. Often we would picnic by streams and Philip would build dams. One day when we were having a lunch-time drink, some Morris men gave a display and Peter was fascinated by the music and their colourful dancing.

We also visited my parents in North Yorkshire and were able to enjoy a mixture of seaside and hills. Peter has taken a long time to respond to other people, but seeing his grandparents regularly has meant that he came to know them well. My mother would look after him for days or part of a day, and by doing everything for him, felt close to him. My father's big knee always seemed a particu-larly welcome place for Peter to sit when he was small, and later on, when he could walk, he would always direct Papa to his chair, as if that was where he should remain! It was a pity that Andy's parents were at the other end of the country and were unable to have the same contact.

When we were at home in Durham, we were able to take walks by the river and play cricket and football with Philip on the school field, with Peter watching. The nine week break passed all too quickly.

When the autumn term started, our days were again very busy. Philip was moving into the reception class and out all day. For the second year I was teaching eight periods a week at my husband's school, at times when he was able to look after Peter. Looking back, we would wonder how we managed to box and cox in that way. We decided that it was thanks to the long evenings. As the boys were still going to bed early, this gave us a quiet time to gather our thoughts, so that we could keep up the hectic pace of each day. I personally found the teaching a godsend, particularly during the difficult months of Peter's infant spasms, as it obliged me to turn my mind to the A-level history syllabus and the needs of my pupils, rather than focusing all the time on our problems.

We come again into the brown hall. Zena greets me. She is pleased to see me. 'Hello Peter, are you better?' Mummy carries me across the room to join her friends. She sits me down on her knee. Some children are on the floor. I watch. I am put down to join them. A ball comes towards me, I push it with my hand, as my brother has taught me. I do it again. Then I find a red tin, I grab it and bang, it makes lovely sounds. Mummy does not think so. 'Drinks time, Peter, come and sit down.' She puts me on a small chair by a little table. I quickly drink my orange and eat my biscuit. There is a little girl on the chair next to me. She is looking round. She doesn't eat her biscuit, I pick it up and eat it. She cries. Mummy is cross. Zena finds another biscuit for Clare. The children are looking at me. A helper comes and takes me to the book corner and shows me pictures. After a while, I am returned to Mummy. 'We must go Peter, I have some shopping to do before tea.'

The buggy bumps its way down the street, cars come very close, I see their wheels, the wheels of the lorry are bigger than me. We go into a little shop, there is a queue. I can see legs, skirts, trousers, my eyes feel heavy. There is a click as the front door opens. I wish we were still outside. I like the sounds of the river, the bustle of people, the musicians on the bridge. Why are we home already? I cry.

'Oh Peter, why couldn't you sleep a little longer and let me cook the tea. Come on out of your buggy. Don't be so upset.' Mummy cuddles me. In the kitchen, she turns on some music. Gradually, the beautiful sounds penetrate my sobbing. I begin to feel calmer. Mummy sits me on the floor beside my toy television. She rushes round getting the meal . . .

We continued to go to occupational therapy sessions with the Down's group at Earl's House each week. We also went to the local mother and toddler group which met on two afternoons. It was very fortunate that Zena, who ran it, was the mother of a boy with Down's Syndrome about five years older than Peter and so she was very understanding. We had known her from Philip's days at toddler club. It was an opportunity for Peter to mix with normal children, while I enjoyed chatting with the other mums. They all took an interest in Peter's progress, to the extent that one helper remarked that she was glad to see Peter so much better, as when we had first joined a few months previously, she hadn't thought he would survive! I was somewhat flabbergasted by that statement, but realised she wanted to encourage me about how much Peter had improved since his illness! Above all, I appreciated the toddler club because Peter was able to participate on fairly equal terms in a normal everyday situation. Opportunities for this grew less as he grew older.

Plain walls again. I am in a strange cot. I play with my bluebird. The curtains are bright. There are engines, so many colourful engines. A nurse fetches us. Mummy carries me into a different room. There are many interesting objects, knobs, wires, screens in this new room. I wish I could explore them. 'Be a brave boy, Peter, I am going to give you a little prick,' says the nurse. I feel sleepy . . .

I recognise this rolling countryside, but it's different. It's no longer purple with the heather. It is brown, stark, less friendly. It seems to go on for ever, but no, these houses are familiar. We stop. 'Hello Peter, have you come to Goathland to see Nana?' 'Hello Pedro.' I like it here, I am special. They put me on the floor by the toys. Why stay still? In the corner, I can see bright pictures moving. I crawl over to see them more closely and to be near the sound. Large hands grab me. 'No Peter, you play! I am back by the box of toys. I'll try again. I get close, the sounds invade me. Hands are placed round me. 'You must sit still Peter. Don't get so near the television, no one else can see.' Once more, I am set down by the toy box. What else can I explore? If I look in another corner, I can see a tree; I don't remember seeing one there before. Brightly coloured lights shine on it, small objects glisten. I must get nearer. I crawl over. I touch a blue light, it is warm. I pull a branch. There is a tinkling sound. I do it again. I am picked up. 'No, Peter, you'll break the decorations.' . . .

We are surrounded by boxes, with coloured paper. I like the paper, it is rustling; if I throw it, it twirls as it lands. 'Look at this present from cousin John' they say . . .

'Thank you, Philip and Peter, for making our Christmas' say Nana and Papa, as we drive away.

We were jolted out of any real sense of security in September, when Peter was taken into the Freeman hospital for two days so that he could have an echo-cardiograph while under sedation, to establish the nature of his hole in the heart. I stayed in with him and, during the tests, watched while strange patterns showed up on the

the screen. The consultant whom we had known since Peter was three months old and who felt like a friend, kept me informed about what they were finding out. Peter would need surgery when he was about five years old for a partial atrio ventricular septal defect. Then came the bombshell. The consultant said he believed that he had told me about the varying policies in different hospitals with regard to heart surgery for the mentally handicapped, and that he would see Peter had an operation even if it meant going to London. I found myself saying that Peter was valuable to us even if he wasn't to others. Later on the same evening he called me into his office for a chat saying that he had seen my face that afternoon! He then amplified what he had said earlier explaining that, while some hospitals operated according to need, others had restricted lists, because of costs and therefore gave priority to normal and younger people, while a third group declined to operate on the handicapped. At that stage, the Freeman fell into the second category, but as its cardiothoracic unit was developing fast, it was likely that, by the time Peter needed surgery, its policy would have changed and he could be a patient there. The doctor told me something of the dilemmas of doctors faced with older handicapped people needing operations, and cared for by ageing parents. If given a new lease of life, they might then outlive their parents and be very unhappy if they had to go into an institution, having always lived at home. He believed society wanted doctors to play God.

I was grateful for the time he had given me. I was nonetheless devastated. How could handicapped people be denied a life-saving operation? How was it that we lived in a society where life could become unbearable for a handicapped person on the death of his or her parents? I felt as if I had been duped. So far I had been impressed by the help I had received, as if everything possible was being done to further Peter's development and then, suddenly, when it was a matter of his fundamental well-being, there was a question mark over the way society would respond to his need!

I hardly slept that night, as I turned over in my mind what I had learnt and realised that, in some people's eyes, Peter counted for less than his normal peers. When I returned home, I wrote to our Member of Parliament. He was very helpful and contacted the Minister of Health on my behalf, suggesting that I follow the matter up a second time when the first letter skirted over issues. In the end I learnt that the subject was under review and that many decisions had to be left to the doctor's clinical judgement.

In 1982, Peter was operated on at the Freeman hospital very successfully. He received the highest standard of medical treatment and every effort was made to enable him to feel at home on the ward. But, after that revelation in 1978, I began to realise there was a dark and sinister side to the way in which some people regarded the handicapped, and I realised that it was not just a case of fighting for better services, but also for basic rights.

The year finished with a happy Christmas spent in North Yorkshire. In some ways our life seemed to be full of paradoxes, so much to enjoy and yet now there was always the knowledge that Peter was handicapped, not only by his own condition but also by some people's attitudes towards him; an awareness which was later further heightened at the time of the legal actions involving 'Baby Alexandra' and 'Dr Arthur'.

Chapter 5

I CAN WALK!

We come again to the grey solid building at the bottom of the hill. As we open the big door, deep rich sounds invade me. They fill me with joy. I look up at the coloured windows; they shine brightly. I sense a Presence here, it is kindly, it does not frighten me. People sing, people speak. I am carried to the front. The music is louder, I wriggle, I'd like to touch it. My daddy kneels down, I am held tight in his arms. The vicar says, 'The Lord Jesus bless you, Peter' . . .

Peter's third year also was relatively peaceful, at least until the autumn. The same busy weekday routine continued. On Sundays we would all go to church. Peter would spend the first half of the service in the creche being cared for by two teenagers who wanted to nurse and do medicine respectively, while Philip was in Sunday School.

All the children came into the church for the second part of the Eucharist. This seemed to be a happy experience for Peter, who often made kissing noises to express his pleasure. With a large number of small children and a music group with guitars, the level of noise was higher than in many churches and so Peter's joyful sounds were not too obtrusive. Music and stained glass clearly attracted him, and we felt sure he was responsive to the atmosphere; indeed as he grew older his liking for churches became almost a problem! If we passed a church building he would struggle to get out of his push chair, and we would have to hurry by. When our own church was locked, following a theft, he had a tantrum on the doorstep because he could not get into it! His sensitivity to a religious place was uncanny.

We were once visiting Mount Grace Priory in North Yorkshire, and examined the ruins in some details. We looked into the remains of the monastic cells and then came to the area which had been the church. At this point, Peter made his happy kissing noises. Again, on another outing in North Yorkshire we went into a little ancient church in Kirkdale, St. Gregory Minster. It was dusk and there were no lights in the church, yet Peter sat in a pew vocalising his happiness at being there. Religious places seemed to bring him a special joy.

> There is a new boy here today. He is my size. 'This is Peter' they say. 'Hello' he says, as he lines up the cars in the garage, like my brother. 'This is Stuart.' Miss Drummond tells us to go through the red tunnel. Stuart rushes through on all fours. Why go through the tunnel? She puts a musical toy at the other end, it plays a tune. 'Come on Peter, find the music.' 'Go on, Peter' says Mummy pushing me gently. Gradually, I edge my way into the tunnel and crawl through. I grab the music. I don't think I'll do that again . . .

We became increasingly aware that Peter's capacity to play was developing very slowly. Music at all times was a great solace to him and we developed the habit of playing children's tapes a lot of the time. The Fisher-Price musical toys fascinated him, otherwise play was very limited. As he did not appear to imagine situations, his pleasure in small cars or soft toys, for example, was nil.

It was at this stage, through belonging to the Down's children's group at Earl's House, that I also became aware of the diversity in personality and attainment of handicapped children. The little girl, Alison, was a regular mother to her doll, changing and feeding it as if it were her baby! She was fascinating to watch. She had none of

Peter's problems with imaginative play. Again, Stuart, who joined the group at the toddler stage, was beginning to talk and to line up cars in a garage. He was the first Down's child that I had seen whose age almost exactly corresponded with Peter's and yet his achievements were far more advanced. I found this very unsettling as it made me feel I had failed Peter. It also made me wonder about the training programmes that I had followed with a fair measure of determination. Stuart's condition had been diagnosed when several months old and he received no expert advice until he came to Earl's House, but clearly he was doing very well. I remember staying behind at the end of the afternoon to ask Miss Drummond where I had gone wrong. She assured me that I hadn't, that Peter had had, and still had, medical problems to contend with and pointed out that handicapped children are as diverse as normal ones. I found it a hard lesson to learn that Peter was falling behind some of his handicapped peers.

As handicapped people are often stereotyped, so are their parents, and yet, on closer acquaintance, they too are a very diverse group. Some want contact with others with similar problems while others want to keep their situation as normal as they can. Some almost fight the handicap with a fierce determination that their child shall have as normal a level of achievement as possible.

Although parents may differ in their responses, they do have a powerful bond between them, in that they know what it is like to have a handicapped child. This no outsider, however sensitive, can fully understand. When Peter was a few weeks old and before I felt I could cope with a big parents' group, I was introduced by our health visitor to another mother with a Down's daughter. We became good friends and were able to share our concerns for our children, especially as they both had heart conditions. Occasionally we would have tea together. Karen was five when we first knew her. It impressed Philip considerably that she cried bitterly on our departure after our first visit and wanted to come with us! She was a very sociable little girl. She was forever wishing to visit a neighbour's mobile home believing it to be an ice-cream van! In the end she had to be allowed to inspect it in order that she could appreciate the difference.

When I was asked to visit a young mother whose first child had Down's Syndrome and a severe heart condition, we found we spoke the same language. It is an unusual experience to meet a stranger and to be able to discuss immediately very deep and personal matters. Peter made that possible.

My daddy holds my hands, I feel safe. I stand up. 'Walk towards me, Peter.' I look down at my blue boots, I take a tentative step. I look at my foot as it moves forward. 'Good boy, Peter.' I move my other foot forward. I throw myself forward into daddy's waiting arms, and he throws me in the air. Then his safe arms are around me again. 'You'll walk soon, Peter' . . .

I have never seen this room before. I have a different cot, it is brown. There is a bed for Philip. I stand up, I make my bluebird play my tune, I shake the sides of my cot, again and again. Mummy comes in, 'We'll go for a drive. It will help you to feel sleepy.' I've never been in the car in my pyjamas before. It is very exciting. We go into the hills, the sky is streaked pink, it is beautiful. I laugh. I shout. I am returned to my cot. 'I'll never do that again' says my mummy . . .'

I awake, I look round this strange room, I stand up. Philip sleeps, curled up in his bed. I wish I had something to play with. I see my bluebird on the ground. I can't reach it, I lean over, further and further. I am falling fast, I hit the ground. My head throbs and hurts, my eyes close. I am in my mother's arms. She repeats and repeats 'Stay awake, Peter, please stay awake.' Her voice sounds funny. A doctor is here, he looks in my eyes. 'I think he is all right. I'll call back later' . . .

We are on a lovely expanse of grass. In the distance, there are rough stone walls, flowers grow out of them. Philip rushes around with his sword. I would like to join him. I stand. Will I fall? I wobble slightly. I take a step towards by brother and then another. He comes towards me. 'Peter's walking,' he cries. 'Well done, Peter!' He gives me a hug and I sit down with a bump.

The most exciting development for us in Peter's third year was that he walked unaided. We remember it very clearly as we had rented a bungalow in the Yorkshire Dales at the time. Children with Down's Syndrome tend to walk late, because of the floppiness of their limbs. We felt that at two and a half Peter had reached a landmark. I think he did too, as he grinned widely as he toddled along.

That holiday was memorable for several reasons, not least our enjoyment of the beautiful countryside and historic ruins. Philip made himself a meccano sword and charged around castles and monasteries alike, waving it.

The middle Sunday of the fortnight brought us one of the several scares that Peter had given us in his lifetime. He managed to fall out of his cot on to his head in his anxiety to reach a favourite toy It was in the early morning and we were awakened by an enormous thud from the other bedroom. We rushed in to find Peter lying pale and floppy on the floor by his cot. I picked him up and his eyes seemed to roll and flicker as if he was going to black out completely. My husband rushed to the neighbours to ask them to ring for a doctor. It was only 6am, but fortunately they were awake as they had small children and the doctor was with us within twenty minutes, by which time Peter was beginning to look more normal. The doctor called round again late that morning to satisfy himself that Peter was completely all right.

It had seemed a good idea to keep Peter in a cot for a long time, as we had believed he was safe there and also because he was an extremely restless sleeper. It then became imperative to put him in a bed, but we had to use a couple of bed sides so that it was difficult for him to roll out. We were lucky at home that the doors had old-fashioned knobs which Peter could not open so that we believed him to be safe in his room; but as we had two sets of stairs, each had to have a gate at the top.

It was becoming a problem that Peter was growing in size but that his understanding of his environment did not match his physical development.

Chapter 6

I AM SAD

The same four walls, the same toys. I play my drum. Mummy puts my record player in front of me, I hear the same tune, I push it away. I cry, I feel angry, I can't contain myself. Everything wells up inside me. It pushes me forwards. My head touches the ground again and again. I hurt myself.

I sob. Mummy picks me up. 'Don't do that, Peter, *please* don't.'

I have come down a dark passage. I am in the hall. There are so many children, but no mummies. No Zena. They are my size, these children, they seem so brave. Two boys are climbing a frame, a girl rushes past me on a trike. Mummy walks me across the room. I climb on her knee, I huddle against her, it is so noisy. The children beside us are drawing lovely pictures, they are so clever. I don't like it here, I begin to cry . . .

In the autumn of 1979, Peter's frustration became a real problem. On occasions, he had always had the capacity to become upset, particularly in the days of his afternoon sleep when he would often wake up distressed; a walk in his pushchair would pacify him or music would eventually soothe him. However, it now seemed very difficult to please him for any length of time. We had had such a good summer holiday that this new phase came as something of a shock. Even his favourite musical toys seemed to annoy him. As I was teaching for one and a half hours on each of four mornings, our opportunities for mixing with other children were more restricted than they might otherwise have been; he needed to be content at home, which he clearly was not. Attempts to introduce more varied activities—building bricks, scribbling, etc.—were met with fierce refusals. Even when we went out, we could not be sure he would be happy. At the Earl's House sessions he seemed frustrated and, as they occurred in the afternoon, he was often tired and grumpy. I had the feeling of inadequacy that I could not please him. I felt a failure in that I seemed unable to help him to develop. He was angry and unpredictable.

I then had to consider ways of helping him to vary his time. I had always wanted him to mix with normal children and harboured hopes that he might go to playgroup and the nursery class at the infant school attended by Philip. I had spoken to the headmistress when he was tiny, who had promised to consider the matter very seriously provided that she could get extra help from County Hall, and that it was on the recommendation of the educational psychologist. We knew that he could go to the nursery unit at the special school; we had visited it and found it very caring, but it would take him out of the normal environment. I therefore got into contact with the playgroup leader who had looked after Philip and who, as it happened, had experience with handicapped children; she was happy to try to accommodate him. We went along together, but, on two counts, Peter could not cope with the situation. At certain times there was a fairly high level of noise which distressed him, and the children were way ahead of him in their activities.

Mummy and Daddy put me in my car seat. We drive towards the edge of the town. We stop outside a long low building. Daddy carries me inside. 'So this is Peter,' says a bright lady. 'Come in I'll show you round.' We go along a corridor, there are big pictures of trees with orange leaves on the wall. We look into classrooms. 'Hello,' say the children. We go outside into another building on its own. The children are nearer my size. 'Hello, Peter,' says a slim lady with a kind voice, 'have you come to visit us again? Would you like a ride on a rocking horse? Is that nice, Peter?' I smile, I like it here. I wish I could stay longer, but we have to go home . . .

A man has come into our house, he looks at me

hard. 'Hello, Peter', he says. Mummy sits me at the table. He opens a black case. I wonder why. He places three bricks in front of me, one yellow, one red, one green. 'Make a tower for me, Peter' he says. I swoosh the bricks on the floor—that *is* fun. He gets them back and places them in front of me. I put one on top of the other, and then on to the floor they go again!

I was forced to realize that Peter was only going to get the help he needed in the context of the special school. Had he been less handicapped, my dreams of integrating him into a normal playgroup nursery and infant school would have been feasible, but he had to have expert help. Having made the decision we asked Dr Robertshaw, the consultant psychiatrist, if she could set the wheels in motion. The educational psychologist, who had visited Peter several times since his birth, came to the house and carried out tests. These were always rather tense times as I hoped Peter would do his best but knew that it was very unlikely that he would co-operate! In this instance, his unwillingness to comply with the tasks was perhaps advantageous as it underlined the need for special education! The community clinician gave her approval and Peter was able to visit the school for several mornings at the end of the autumn term and was ready to start school, mornings only, in the spring term.

I spent a couple of sessions at the nursery unit with Peter, while he became accustomed to his new environment, and was very pleased with what I saw. The building was modern and set apart from the main school. It accommodated up to eight children. Peter was the youngest. The oldest children were seven and waiting to move up into the next class. Mrs Ferguson, the teacher, had enormous patience and great affection for the children. She was very experienced and firm in the kindest way possible. A welfare assistant worked with her. Much of the time had to be spent on routine matters like regular toiletting, but each child had his own work programme and there were times of communal play or singing. I felt considerable relief that someone else was going to bear some of the responsibility for helping Peter to develop. It was as if an enormous burden had been lifted from our shoulders.

Chapter 7

MY NURSERY CLASS

In my classroom we have bright toys. I like the musical radio. I play it. The other lady winds it up for me again and again. Then my teacher takes me to the special corner. I sit on a small chair. She places her finger under my chin. 'Look at me, Peter.' Fleetingly my eyes catch her blue ones. I see the light in them. 'Good boy, Peter'. She sounds pleased. 'Look at me, Peter.' I look at the mirror; in it I can see the table. 'Look at me, Peter.' I look again quickly. 'Good boy, Peter Morgan.' I like it when she says that.

We all sit down together and have a drink and then my teacher sings to us. We try to copy the way her arms move. Craig is good at that.

Here is my mummy again. I smile at her. I have enjoyed my morning. 'He certainly knows his mum' says my teacher.

Although we had always tried to help Peter's progress, we appreciated that teachers could adopt a systematic professional approach. The first skill that Peter was taught was to look someone in the eye. We had been aware that Peter avoided eye contact, but had not known how to remedy it! Mrs Ferguson, by gently placing her hand under his chin and saying, 'Look at me, Peter', and then saying 'good boy', when he did so, however fleetingly, was teaching a skill in a way that had eluded us. Peter still does not meet our eyes as much as a normal child would, but his eye contact has gradually improved.

As well as an individual work programme, school provided Peter with a variety of activities: waterplay, singing, looking at books, times in the garden, swimming. It also gave him friends.

'We must meet Philip.' Mummy puts me in my buggy, and we walk fast, down the bumpy path towards the river, alongside the water and up by the church and to the school. Lots of people stand outside. It is very crowded. Some children rush out waving paintings, not my brother. It is noisy. Mummy is talking. I want to move again, to go back on the river banks. I cry. Mummy lifts me out of my push chair and holds me. I cry and cry. 'Here is Philip.' She sounds relieved. She puts me in my buggy and starts pushing me. I stop crying. I like my ride.

For the first two terms I would fetch Peter from school at lunch time and we'd spend the afternoon together. He was often tired which didn't always make them easy times, but we would shop, or go for walks or play and end up meeting his brother from school. Sometimes we would have friends to tea.

Philip has gone off to school today. Everyone is bustling around. My bag is in the hall. I must be going too. Yes, Mummy puts me in the car. I am pleased to see my nursery again. My teacher gives a warm welcome. 'Hello, Peter Morgan.' Why am I always Peter Morgan at school? Here are my friends standing round. Here are the familiar toys. The work table is in the corner. If I go and sit there, perhaps Mrs Ferguson will play with me first.

'Peter is keen today' says my teacher. 'I wonder if he can still point to the cup, the car and the brush?' 'Well done, Peter.' We play, have a drink, sing songs. Where is Mummy? She doesn't come. Food has arrived. Mrs Ferguson puts an apron on me.

'You are going to stay for dinner with us,' she says.

We sit down at our table. A bowl of potatoes, sausages and peas is placed in front of me. A helper sits beside me. She takes my spoon and fills it with food. She takes my hand and places it on the handle. She guides it to my mouth. The food is nice. We do this again and again. 'Good boy' says my helper. 'You can have your pudding now.' When my mummy comes much later they say I have enjoyed my day.

We have to drive fast to collect my brother from school. I am glad to sit quietly in the car, while Mummy stands by the gate.

In the autumn of 1980, we decided that Peter should go to school full-time. I remember well feeling very desolate on the first day of the term. After eight years of spending a lot of time in the company of my small boys, I had the hours from 9.30—3.00 to myself! Nevertheless, going to school provided a more satisfying way of life for Peter. He was much happier for being there and I soon adjusted.

Today my classroom looks different. There are big pictures on the wall. The table has been moved. 'Hello Peter'. Where is Mrs Ferguson? Why is Mrs Watson here? 'Shall we hang up your coat, Peter? I'm your teacher now.'

In September 1981, there was a reshuffle of staff at Southview. Since the children stay for several years in the same classroom, it was decided to move the teachers, to provide a change. Peter's new teacher was recently trained, and very professional. She too became a good friend to him, to the extent that she was as concerned as any member of the family when he had his heart operation and came to visit him in hospital and when he was convalescing. She was bright and positive and seemingly unflappable.

Peter did not forget Mrs Ferguson and when I took him to school in the morning, he would slip into the special care class at the end of the main building, if he possibly could, to be greeted and to play with the musical toys. I was reluctant to let him do this too often, as he was sometimes difficult to dislodge.

Mrs Watson is putting on our coats. We don't go far, just into the big school. I hurry along the passage. 'Hello, Peter Morgan' calls Rosie. I don't stop. I want to get to the hall. We have music there. Mrs Wynn is already sitting at the piano. I go up to her. 'Hello, Pete, you go and sit by Sarah.' I'd rather stand by the piano. Mrs Watson takes me firmly by the hand. She sits beside me. Sarah is on the other side. She is my special friend. More children come in. Mrs Wynn starts to play 'Little Donkey.' I like this one . . .

There was a warm family atmosphere in the school, typical of the north-east. There were approximately sixty children aged between three and nineteen. They would meet up regularly for singing sessions. There would be end-of-term discos, concerts and parties, and so the children got to know those who were not in their class. Those who could talk would greet the other children loudly. Peter was always 'Peter Morgan' at school. He loved going into the main building and would expect that it was singing each time, although in fact it could equally be soft play or one of the regular medical inspections!

Parents also felt part of the school community. For the first couple of years I took Peter in our car, since Andy didn't need it, and he did seem very small at three to be transported. It also meant that I could chat to the staff, and find out what he had been doing each day. Nonetheless I felt that he must gradually become more independent and from the age of five and a half, he went by taxi. There was no problem as he enjoyed the car ride and the company. Mrs Watson and I then exchanged notes in a newsbook, and I could still visit the school whenever I needed. There was also a variety of social activities arranged by the Parent/Teacher Association which were well supported by the parents, and provided a valuable link with the teachers. The activities also often involved fund-raising. In an area of high unemployment this was necessary, to enable outings and holidays to take place. Important items were also purchased, for example a soft play area was set up, a kitchen was fitted out, a minibus was bought, even a static caravan in Weardale was acquired, to be used by the older children and also families in the holidays. We all enjoyed being part of Peter's school.

Chapter 8

I LIKE THAT TUNE

It has been our constant wish to enable Peter to develop to his full potential. As Peter became established at school, we wanted to provide him with one or two outside interests. Music had always been a great passion in his life and, rather by chance, we found that this was something upon which we could build.

Mummy is tidying up. Someone is coming to see us. When the bell rings, we all go to the front door. A lady is standing there. 'Hello Philip, hello Peter.' 'This is Dr Urquhart,' says Mummy. I like the doctor's voice. She comes with us into the kitchen. Soon, shrill sounds fill the room. She is holding something long and brown to her mouth. I move close to touch it. She stops playing. 'Do you like my recorder?' She plays again. She then starts to sing, 'If you're happy and you know it, clap your hands . . .' My brother joins in. Dr Urquhart pushes my hands together. She talks to Mummy. I feel tired. I feel confused. I begin to cry. Mummy holds me. I still cry. 'He has had enough for today,' says Dr Urquhart.

. . . We are driving towards school, but we turn off the big road . . . we stop outside a bungalow, my friend comes to meet us. Mummy carries me up the steps and through the front door. We go into a room which is filled with something enormous and black. My friend leads me over to it. She sits on a stool. Her fingers go fast over the keys. I hear the rich sounds. It is like the piano at school, but much bigger.

If you're happy and you know it, clap your hands. I place my hands together.

'Well done' says Dr Urquhart. 'Clever boy.' I want to get close. She takes me on her knee and places my hands on top of hers. Our hands race up and down together.

The wheels of the bus go round and round . . .

'Now you and Mummy must play' says Dr Urquhart.

Mummy sits me on a chair, and places a hammer in each of my hands. She holds my fists. Together we hit the bars, in front of me. They chime loudly. Dr Urquhart begins to play. *Put on the skillet* she sings. Mummy and I play the tune, too. I'd like to do it louder. My mother seems to be stopping me . . .

'I think he has done very well for the first time here' says Dr Urquhart. 'Is it time to take him to school?'

Margaret Urquhart came into our lives when I was given her name as someone who might talk to a group of parents about music therapy. She mentioned that she would like to work with a handicapped child. I asked her if she would teach Peter.

Initially Margaret came to our house on a Saturday morning. Our piano needed attention and so, as soon as she had got to know Peter, she suggested that we come to her home which was on the way to the school. Between 8.45 and 9.15 each Tuesday, Peter and I would stop off at her bungalow. He would sit on her knee and put his hands on the backs of hers and they would play her grand piano together. He and I would perform the actions to songs. She taught him to sing 'La' on C, although having done it several times he refused to repeat the performance, as if to say that was enough. He and I would play a glockenspiel.

As he got to know Margaret, Peter became quite bossy and, on his arrival, would lead her to the piano, push her on to the stool and place her hands on the keys. His little body would tense in excitement and a big grin would spread across his face as she began to play. She became one of Peter's greatest friends.

As I am pushed across the grass, I hear lovely sounds, rich and piercing and clear. We all stop. Mummy spreads a rug on the ground. She and Daddy and Philip sit down. 'You stay in your buggy, Peter.' The tunes dance inside my head. They make me happy. Why do they stop? I want them to go on for ever. I want them to play again. I cry and crash my head against the buggy. 'The band needs a break, Peter, come on get out of your buggy and have a run round.' I head off towards the band as fast as I can. Perhaps they will play for me again.

'Hello Peter, would you like me to play?' but Daddy grabs me. He talks to the man. Soon the players are going back to the seats. 'We'll go back to Mummy, Pete.'

As I hear the tunes again I can smile once more . . .

In the summer, there were brass-band concerts on the grass beside County Hall, Durham, and sometimes we would walk up there. Peter was fascinated by the music and would tense himself in his excitement. We had to keep him in his buggy as otherwise he would have gone as close to the instruments as possible. The only problem was his inability to understand that the players needed a break, and he became very distressed when they stopped playing. On one occasion during the interval he beetled off to see the instruments very quickly, and we were fortunate that, on that particular Sunday, his teacher's husband was one of the players. He came and talked to Peter.

Outside the shop there is a lady playing. People in brightly coloured clothes and noisy shoes dance. My daddy stops close by. The tunes make me glad. I like to see the fast moving feet, the clashing of sticks, the sound of bells . . .

The music stops. The lady comes over to me. 'Would you like to play?' I press the keys. I like the sounds. She talks to me and Mummy and Daddy.

Our holidays in Whitby often coincided with the Folk Festival and we would find musicians and dancers in many parts of the town at various times of the day. Peter loved this. The combination of music and movement was a delight to him. His pleasure was so apparent that sometimes the performers would stop and speak to him. On one occasion he was allowed to 'play' the accordeon.

We always felt that had the Pied Piper arrived, Peter would have been the first to follow him without a backward glance! His love for music was almost uncanny. His tastes are catholic: pop music, children's tunes, brass bands and classical pieces all appealed to him. On one occasion he sat for half an hour by the television for a Horowitz recital, quite an achievement for a six year old! He does require that the tunes are bright and will turn off the cassette player if he considers the music insufficiently lively. He also has his favourite tapes and will listen to them again and again in preference to a wide variety. We have always felt that his love of music is one of the greatest compensations for his handicaps. It gives him enormous pleasure and has soothed him when he has been distressed.

Chapter 9

MY FRIENDS

Some children of my size are seated at tables. They have crayons and paper.

My friend Juliet says 'Hello Peter'. I sit on a small chair. She sits beside me. She puts a brightly coloured box in front of me. There are books in it. We look at one together. I want to get up and look around the room. 'No, sit down, Peter, we'll find another book' says Juliet.

The children are putting their crayons away.

We all take our chairs and put them near the piano. I would like to touch it. 'No sit down, Peter' says Juliet.

The children sing

The wise man built his house upon the rock.

The wave their arms up and down. Juliet takes my hands and moves them too.

Another way in which we sought to create opportunities for Peter was by getting him involved in the Sunday School, which was available at our church to children when they were five years old. Before that, they attended a creche. Peter's last couple of years in the creche were not particularly satisfactory as the teenage girls who had been particularly interested in him had gone to college and more often than not I would stay and look after him myself. I did want him to have some independence from me and also to mix with his peers.

The Sunday School was run by two very capable and caring mothers, Barbara and Joy, who were happy to take Peter as long as I could give them some help in the activities that would interest him. I told them that he liked books and very simple jig-saws, that he loved music, but that he didn't follow a story nor could he draw. We therefore worked out a compromise by which I would bring him late to the Sunday School, after the other children had had their talk and were engaged in activities. He would have a box with things that were particularly appropriate for him to play with and the session would end with singing. Joy had a daughter Juliet who wanted to work with children and who had already met Peter, and so she would supervise him. Eventually Peter was able to be present for

the whole session and the teachers said they were grateful
to him for making them think about the musical content
of their classes. There was also one occasion at least when
Peter coming in late with a wide grin on his face, cheered
everyone up. When Juliet was away another girl, Denise,
helped Peter and I now appreciate just how fortunate we
were.

When Peter was eight we moved from Durham, and we
have not been able to make such an ideal arrangement
since.

My friends come up to me. They smile. They
push a parcel in my hands. What do I do with it?
'Happy birthday', they say. 'That's lovely, thank
you' says Mummy and takes off the brightly
coloured paper. A small red bus. What shall I do
with it? My brother seems very excited. He is bigger
than the other children. They like him. 'Let's go on
the slide' he says. They follow him up and down
the slide. Daddy puts me on the slide and the
ground rushes towards me. I like it, but I would
rather sit and watch the other children. 'Shall we
play 'the farmer's in his den'?' I am pushed in the
middle. They pat me. I am not sure I like this very
much. I sit down.

We rush downstairs for tea. In the middle of the
table is a large cake. Mummy lights the candles.
My brother draws the curtains across. I like watching the bright flames. My brother blows them out.
Everyone sings 'Happy birthday.' I like my tea. I
like my friends.

I did fear that once Peter was at special school, he would have too little contact with normal children, and I think that this has indeed been the case. We have tried to remedy this as far as possible. Each year he has had a birthday party with a small group of children which has always been an enjoyable occasion. Peter hasn't always been happy to go into other people's homes and this has created a further difficulty in trying to get him to mix with others.

We have collected my brother from school. Another lady and her little boy have come to our car. We set off for home, then we turn up the hill. We stop outside a house. Mummy lifts me out. I don't wish to be here. I should be at home. I do not know this room. I cry. Mummy sits me on her knee. She gives me a toy. I push it away, I don't want to be here. Food is put on the table. I still cry. I push the plate away.

My brother is happy. He and Robert play with the cars. He eats a lot of tea.

'I think we had better go home' says my mother. 'I am sorry Peter hasn't settled.'

We get in the car. I am happy. I stop crying.

We did have to recognize that in some instances we had to move very slowly as we encouraged Peter to break out of his own world. Going to his own school, to Dr Urquhart, to church and Sunday School, or on outings were usually happy experiences for him. Occasionally he would be upset, but not always. Visiting unfamiliar homes was another matter, particularly at the end of a school day when presumably he was tired and just wished to follow his normal routine. On several occasions he set up a howl on arrival, which ceased miraculously when we got into the car to go home an hour or two later! In one instance, although outwardly happy and interested in exploring the room, he refused to eat any tea despite his liking for food.

We tried to overcome the problem of his insecurity in strange environments by persisting in taking him out when invited, otherwise there was a danger that we would stay at home because it was the easiest path to take! I talked over these difficulties with Mrs Ferguson who suggested that we should go to houses for short periods of time to start with, if we could. I tried to do this, calling on friends for twenty minutes or so, so that Peter could get used to going into different homes. We could take comfort that he felt none of these inhibitions about visiting Anna, who lived next door but one, and was a couple of years younger than he. We regularly had tea at each others's homes and Peter felt very secure. Indeed I can remember when we called on the off chance one day to find no one at home, that Peter had a paddy on the doorstep, so unhappy was he that he could not get in!

Peter certainly wasn't typical of the stereotype of the sociable Down's boy and served to show that it is impossible to generalise. Certainly some children with Down's Syndrome are far more outwardgoing and sociable. Karen was one example. So was a little girl on Whitby beach whom we got to know. She would visit everyone sitting near her, and was a great contrast to Peter. She was also fascinated by water, and would dash to the sea whenever possible!

Chapter 10

I MUST GET NEAR THE BELLS

There is a difficult balance to be achieved for families with a mentally handicapped child. It is that between encouraging them to be independent and keeping them safe. Sometimes mothers of handicapped children are castigated for being over protective, but others point out that if they are, it is nature's way of looking after the helpless. There may well be a tendency to be too cautious, but it is understandable when the dangers are many.

The bells are pealing. The chimes invade me. The tunes excite me. I want to be closer, closer beside the bells, to be part of their music. How can I get nearer? I climb on the radiator, on to the window sill. I reach up and catch hold of the top of the window. My fingers curl round and grasp the frame, I pull. Nothing moves. I pull harder. The window comes down with a jerk. I can lean out, closer to the bells.

There are hands around my waist. They pull me away from the sounds into the room. 'Oh Peter, you could have been killed!' Mummy holds me tight, she sounds frightened, almost angry. What have I done?

One evening, when Peter was four, the cathedral bell-ringers were practising. He had already gone to his bed, but I heard loud and excited noises coming from his room. I decided to investigate. I found him standing on the windowsill, with the top part of the sash window completely down, leaning out from his waist. He could so easily have toppled out and fallen to the pavement below in his anxiety to get close to the bells.

We were very alarmed and conscience-stricken that he could have incurred such danger. We had neither realised that he could climb like that nor that he had the strength to pull down the window. We thought blocks on the window would solve the problem.

I'm awake. The house is silent. I go to the window. I see the familiar trees. The clock chimes. I turn away and find my drum. I bang it, again and again. Nobody comes. I feel shut in. The clock chimes again. I would like to be outside. I go to the window again. How can I break out? I feel angry, stifled. My head butts the window, hard, harder. Crash! There is a shattering tinkle of glass below. I can see my friend Hugh. He goes away. Mummy is beside me. She puts her hands on my head and guides it back into the room. She cuddles me.

One morning we were awakened by the loud shattering of glass. A minute later we heard our neighbour's voice calling to us that Peter had his head through the window. In fact, the sash window was composed of a number of small panes and, by breaking one of these, Peter had just enough space to push his head through, but there was still jagged glass in the wood. We managed to go to the bedroom without startling Peter and draw his head back, but again he had given us a real scare. Our first thought was to get bars at the window to prevent a recurrence, but when a friend started putting them up he thought they were for climbing and so we quickly abandoned that idea. We had some shatterproof glass put up, with a very small gap left at the top to let some air in. These have been the occasions upon which Peter has exposed himself to the greatest danger, and have made us aware of the need always to check his environment to make sure it is safe for him.

Chapter 11

MY HOLIDAYS

'This is to be our house in the holidays, Peter. This is your bedroom' I do not have to go up any stairs. I cannot see out of the high window. My brother has rushed outside. I follow him. He goes into the garden. There are more children here. They are rushing up and down, chasing a football. I like seeing them. I get in the middle of them. I go this way and that following the ball. It lands at my feet and I push it with my toe . . .

We go to the sea. My daddy puts on my trunks. He carries me to the water. White froth creeps over my toes, it is very cold. My daddy jumps me over the waves, I laugh, but then I begin to shiver. I am cold. I don't like it any more by the sea . . .

My other nana and papa have come to see us. We go out in the car, up hill and down. I like that. Why do we have to stop? There is only greenness. Nothing to look at. I cry. 'I'll take Peter a little walk in his buggy before the picnic', says my mummy. Philip, Daddy and Papa play cricket.

Holidays can be a problem for families with handicapped children. Certainly Peter, as a small child, could not accommodate to the routine of an hotel. He would wake up grumpy, for example, and would need to have his breakfast as soon as possible. Rented accommodation had served our purpose in the previous two years but increasingly, as he became more mobile and adventurous, we would have to be sure that it was suitable for his needs.

As we lived in a school house, our solution was one which obviously is not open to everyone, that is to buy a holiday house. It would also be a safeguard in that we would have somewhere to live in retirement! At first we dreamed of a stone built cottage on the North Yorkshire moors, but rapidly realised that a modern bungalow on a small estate would better serve our purpose. We found one in a large village four miles from the sea. It had the necessary three bedrooms, for it was impossible for the boys to share. Peter would often wake very early and roam around his room, or alternatively go to sleep late. It was also easy to maintain and clean. There were lots of children around for Philip to play with and Peter could join in too. He loved it when they all played football in the garden and he would sit down in their midst or move with them and occasionally touch the ball. With his limited capacity in play and with his lack of speech, he found it difficult to join in fully and, of course, when the children were out in the cul-de-sac on their bikes, Peter could only be there if we were able to go out as well. Otherwise, he would wander off without any awareness of the danger to himself.

The year we moved in was that of Prince Charles' wedding. There was a street party. Long trestle tables and chairs were put out in the road. Everyone provided food and money for souvenirs for the children. Peter seemed to enjoy himself, even if he did eventually wander back to the bungalow. This celebration certainly broke the ice and made us feel at home.

Day follows day. No school, we stay in our bungalow. Hours by the sea, picnics, drives in the car, sitting on the floor by my music . . . Uncle Dick is coming, they say. Do I know Uncle Dick? The room is full of people. Mummy, Daddy, Philip, a tall man, a lady, a boy my size. 'Say hello to Peter, John.' The voice sounds like my daddy's, but no, the man has dark hair, no glasses. 'Will you sit on my knee, Peter?' I let him pick me up. He is so like my daddy when he speaks so how can I be frightened!? 'Let's clap hands, Peter.' I laugh as the palms of his big hands touch mine. I blow kisses. I like my Uncle Dick. I enjoy his visit. It is hot on the beach. I paddle. Uncle Dick plays lots of football. Philip and John race about. I like watching. 'Come on Peter, *you* kick the ball.' Uncle Dick encourages me. John talks to me. I like that. Some children don't talk to me.

'Hello, Peter.' Today John sits beside me in the car, not my brother. We drive across the moors, a long way, eventually stopping by lines and lines of cars. I am put in my buggy and wheeled near a fence. No, it isn't a fence, more like a room with a fence on the front. Something furry moves in front of me and leaps and curls round a branch with its tail. 'Do you like the monkeys, Peter?' says John. We see so many animals, moving, standing, jumping, swimming. In each cage there is something new to look at. I enjoy going out with my cousin John.

Our holidays in North Yorkshire also enabled us to provide Peter with new experiences. We explored the area, went to the beach, visited grandparents and saw my aunt who lived nearby. Often my brother and his wife would come with their two boys and stay at Goathland. Friends occasionally took holidays in the area and we would go out together. The second summer holidays we spent in the bungalow, Andy's brother, his wife and son came for a week to an hotel in Whitby. John was just a couple of months younger than Peter, and with encouragement from his parents, established a nice relationship with his cousin.

We also came into contact with the Whitby Mencap. One day we stopped at a stall they had on the quay and they began talking to us and invited us to Dalewood House, the centre which they had recently established. It was a marvellous example of what could be achieved by parents with a vision. Since there were no services in Whitby and mentally handicapped people had to travel to Scarborough or Teesside, the committee set up a workshop, a gateway club, Saturday club and holiday play scheme. Sometimes Peter was able to join in and enjoyed spending time in the big playroom going on outings, swimming, or horse-riding with them. We were glad that he was gaining new experiences and meeting different people.

Chapter 12

WHERE ARE MUMMY AND DADDY?

We fetch my brother from school, but we don't go straight home. We draw up outside a strange house. Mummy gets out and knocks on the door. A small lady comes out with her coat on and gets in the car beside Mummy.

'This is Philip. This is Peter.' 'Hello boys,' she says. My brother says 'hello' brightly. I think he likes her voice. He grins broadly. 'You must call me Betty' she says.

Once we arrive home we go straight to the kitchen. The tea is laid. I sit in my place. Betty is beside Philip. She only has a cup of tea. I like a lot for my tea. We all are happy with Betty here. After tea Philip keeps taking toys to show her. I walk up to her. 'Hello Tiger' she says. I've never been called tiger before. Mummy carries me upstairs so that we can show Betty my room.

'What a lovely room, Peter. I'd love to look out on trees!

We did also have to think about our own needs. If one person in the family requires more attention than everyone else, it is possible for relationships to become distorted. We had tried to go out for occasional evenings since Peter was born, but when he was about four, we seemed to run into real problems over baby-sitters. The daughters of the school bursar and the helpers from the crêche had been great stand-bys, but they had all gone to college. We had good friends who would baby-sit if asked, but we did not like to impose upon them regularly. We needed sitters who were known to Peter and familiar with his ways.

I mentioned our dilemma to the health visitor, who asked for time to think, then introduced us to Betty, a delightful widow who helped at a disabled club. She was a gem. I remember waking up on the morning following her visit to the boys as if a great load had been removed from my shoulders. She proved to be like a third 'granny' and I never had any qualms leaving them with her once a month or so. Later Juliet and one or two other teenagers also helped us so that the problem of baby-sitters receded.

What about the need for a longer break? When there is a child with special needs in the family, the parents do have to have the opportunity to recharge their batteries and also to be together so that their own relationship can remain close. When Peter was one and a half years old, my mother looked after both boys for five days while we had a holiday in the Lake District. On this occasion I found it difficult to leave the boys and every time I saw a small child on the first couple of days I felt homesick. It wasn't easy to part from the children and yet it did give us the chance to walk miles across the fells and talk together. Handicapped children can be physically very tiring which can make it difficult for grandparents to look after them as they get older. With my father becoming less well, my mother was not able to stay and look after the boys again, but she often had them both, or Peter alone, for a day when we were in North Yorkshire in the holidays in subsequent years. Thus we were still occasionally able to pursue our hobby and have some time for each other and also for Philip.

Peter then went away with his school to Whitby for five days. I felt secure in the knowledge that his teacher understood all his little ways, though again I found it a wrench to part with him. We tried to make these few days special, even though they were in term-time, and went out in the evening. I could not get over how much more time I had available, when I did not have to give constant attention to Peter.

'So this is Peter. Hello, Peter.'

A lady with rosy cheeks and bright blue eyes is smiling at me. She has a black cloth on her head. 'Say goodbye to Mummy, Daddy and Philip. Come and find some toys.'

We go into a large room. There's a cupboard in the corner. A girl comes over to me. 'Hello Peter', she says. 'This is Anne' says Sister Mac. 'She'll look after you.'

'Do you like him Peter?' It is a teddy. I push him away. 'Here's a car'. Anne runs it across the floor. I see a musical toy and grab it. 'Do you want me to wind it up, Peter?' says Anne. Now I feel at home. I hold it to my ear. I want to see what lies beyond this room. The passages are long and wide. We go down them, we peer into doors, we climb some stairs, we look in bedrooms. People say 'hello'. The children seem bigger than me. There are lots of grown-ups. We go down some different stairs. I hear more music. We go into the kitchen. There is Sister Mac. 'Hello, Peter. Are you getting to know everybody?'

I go and stand by her radio 'Oh you like my music.'

'We'll have dinner soon. Perhaps Peter would like the records on, Anne. Why don't you take him along to the lounge?' At dinner I sit by Anne and she puts meat and vegetables on my plate, and piles the food on my spoon. I look round. There are lots of people in here.

After dinner Anne puts me in my buggy and she pushes me down the street. There are lots of cars going by. She buys some sweets in the shop. She gives me some. I push them away. 'Don't you like sweets, Peter?'

Soon after our return Mummy and Daddy and Philip come to collect me.

'Where are you, Peter?' calls Sister Mac. 'He's been fine. Let him stay overnight next time.'

It was through Peter's headmistress that I took steps to get regular breaks for us. She took a great interest in the whole family, and kept telling me that I owed it to my husband and my son to have some time for them. She knew a remarkable nun who had been a teaching colleague and who was opening a short stay home for the mentally handicapped in Teesside. 'I would leave my own children with her. You can't give a better recommendation than that' she told us.

We decided to go and see Sister Mac, as her friends call her. As we drove over to Middlesbrough, I can well recall the feeling of panic—no, I couldn't leave Peter with strangers. Five minutes in Sister Mac's company removed all qualms. Her warmth of heart and homeliness made my mind easy immediately. After giving us a cup of tea and chatting, she showed us the accommodation. Each bedroom was individually decorated and furnished so that a volunteer and handicapped person could share. That erased one fear that Peter might be left alone and put himself in a dangerous situation. He would be constantly supervised by one of the young Catholic volunteers from the Middlesbrough diocese, whom Sister Mac enrolled and trained. The dining room had been furnished as a result of fund-raising by pool players from a local pub. 'It's like Christmas here' said Sister Mac. 'We keep getting help and gifts.' Above all Sister Mac was practical and we felt that we could, without hesitation, place Peter in her care. Accordingly we filled out a form giving details of his condition and needs and arranged for him to come in for a few hours to get familiar with the place and everyone there. Subsequently Peter stayed for a night and then a couple of nights and gradually we built up to him staying for nine days while we went abroad, when he was seven. In practice it meant that each 'holidays' and half-term he would spend a few nights away and we would mostly stay in North Yorkshire or occasionally, later on, further afield and, as I say, once abroad. Certain helpers got to know him, first Anne, who after a couple of years went away to do mental handicap nursing, and then Gill and, sometimes, Audrey. They have all been marvellous in their concern for Peter and the good relationship they have built with him. As soon as Peter goes into Eston House, he marches to the toy cupboard to find the musical toys and does not take too much notice of us as we say goodbye. When we return, he takes our hand and cannot wait to get into the car. He vocalises loudly as if trying to tell us what he has been doing.

We feel he enjoys his break away. He is involved with more people. He has outings. There are toys, a lovely garden and a soft play room. It is hard to release one's child, but a normal child gains independence by going to his friends' houses and staying with them occasionally, or going to relatives. These opportunities are considerably less for the handicapped child, and therefore they have to be created either by setting up a hostel or organising a short-term fostering scheme.

We have always felt that Peter has benefited from his breaks away and that they have helped him to grow up, to be more independent and to relate better to other people.

We have appreciated our greater freedom and the opportunity to relax together. Because these times have been at intervals, they have been very special. It has also been lovely when we have all been reunited, as it is only then that it feels as if everyone is in their rightful place.

Chapter 13

THE NURSES SAY 'HELLO PETER'

The nurse and Mummy are moving the two beds.
Mine is against the wall, Mummy's is next to it.
There are green and blue engines on the curtains.

We go into a playroom. There is so much to explore. I put the cash register on the table. I press the key, it goes 'ping'. I do it again and again. Mummy makes me sit down with other children. The nurse gives us our dinner. Then, I am whisked away down a long corridor. My mummy takes off my jumper and vest. My chest is pushed against a slab of cold metal. I don't like it. I shout. I wriggle. 'Stay still Peter, just for one moment', says Mummy . . .

A doctor visits us in our room. Again I have to be undressed. He listens to my chest. He talks to Mummy in serious tones. She looks sad. What does it all mean? . . .

Now two ladies in white coats arrive. They wheel a trolley. There are lots of wires on it. They like my music. They sing the tune. Mummy holds me. She lifts up my jumper. Little pads are placed on my chest I don't like them. I want to take them off but Mummy holds my hands tightly. Lines appear on a little screen. There is a whirring noise. One pad is moved, once, twice three times. 'Last time now', says the lady as she places it again on me. 'Good boy'. Why do all these people keep visiting me, making me undress, doing things to me? I just want to lie down on the floor and listen to my music. At last I can.

In October 1983, we received notification that Peter was to have his open-heart surgery at the end of the month. During the next couple of weeks I felt that I was groping my way along a precipice. It was impossible to face with equanimity an operation posing such risks. I knew that if

Peter died, we would be shattered. Then I became increasingly concerned about Peter and myself, living in a strange environment. Would we cope? Would he be disturbed by such a change in his routine? Would he become distressed? I have found that when I am worried about something really serious, my mind often focuses on a more trivial problem, although in this instance, the lesser concern of how Peter would adapt to life in a hospital was real enough.

At this stage, about twelve members from our church were meeting weekly in our home and their support and prayers sustained us when I was full of apprehension, as did the friendship of those around us. Once the time got close, events carried us along.

Andy's mother arrived on the Sunday to look after Philip for a few days, after which we would go and stay with my parents in Goathland for his half term. On the Tuesday, Andy and I took Peter up to the Freeman Hospital. The children's cardiothoracic ward was on the ground floor, light and airy with bright pictures and furnishings. Peter and I were given a small room to share.

One of the first tasks was to rearrange the furniture so that Peter could not fall out of the bed on to the floor! The nurses did everything they could to make us feel at home. Peter was allowed to play his favourite tapes. If they felt he would be happier, they gave him his meals on a tray in our room. Often, ice-cream was produced from the 'fridge for his sweet!

The ECGs, X-rays and visits from doctors did not unduly upset Peter and he settled into his new way of life better than I had dared to hope. The consultant surgeon, anaesthetist and paediatrician individually visited us and, impressing upon us the risks of the operation that was about to be performed, they told us, in layman's terms, what was to happen. I well remember the surgeon saying: 'You have an active child now, but he will not be like this, when he reaches his teens, and that is why he needs to have the operation.'

A nurse pricks my arm. I feel sleepy. I feel peaceful. Mummy and Daddy talk to me. Now I am lifted on to a narrow bed and wheeled along the wide corridors. We come to a door. Mummy and Daddy kiss me.

I go into a strange room, full of people in funny clothes. My eyelids feel heavy . . . how long have I slept? . . . There are lots of voices murmuring around me. Wires seem to be all over me. My chest hurts. I move. Someone takes the tube out of my mouth. I gasp for breath. I make a rasping sound again and again. It hurts. Firm hands hold me. Someone puts a small tube down my throat. I go back to sleep . . .

Once again I hear sounds. It feels as if a long time has passed. The tube is taken from my throat. It doesn't hurt much. My daddy comes and sits beside me. He looks pleased. Soon Mummy is beside him. I give her a big smile . . .

'You will not hear anything for four or five hours, I should go out' was the advice that was given to us, when Peter had been wheeled into the theatre. What do you do while your child undergoes a serious operation? Some parents sit in the ward, unable to drag themselves outside the hospital. Others like ourselves, just want to be alone and so, perhaps rather strangely, we took the Metro up to the coast. Watching the waves break on the shore was calming. The sea seemed so enormous, impersonal, and inexorable in its movements that somehow it made our human worries seem smaller, although no less real. We prayed and prayed for Peter and yet I couldn't help but ask myself why it was we expected Peter to live when we knew that children and babies from that ward did die because of the risks involved in this kind of surgery? Increasingly I was seeing prayer as the surrender of someone into God's hands rather than a request for results.

When we returned to the hospital ward, we heard that the operation had in fact been very successful and that we could visit him in intensive care. We had been allowed to go into intensive care on the previous day so that it would not be too much of a shock to us. It is unnerving to see people attached to so many machines, monitors, drips and gadgets in an intensely clinical atmosphere. In Peter's case he had to be sedated and also had to be given muscle relaxants so that he lay absolutely still. He couldn't be allowed to come round until he was taken off the ventilator as he would not understand why he had to be so quiet.

It was very strange to see him lying so peacefully, and to visit someone so inert. We had been given a room in the nurses' accommodation for the duration of Peter's time in Special Care so that we could both be near him. It was initially expected that this would be for one night, but the first attempt to remove Peter from the ventilator was unsuccessful. It turned out that his respiratory passages were unusually narrow and that they had become swollen. Therefore his throat closed in a spasm when the tube was removed. We were actually present when this happened and were quickly hustled out with offers of cups of tea. About half an hour later we were admitted to the ward again to find Peter again sleeping peacefully, but this time on an infant ventilator with a narrower tube. Additional drugs were being given to him to reduce the swelling in his throat. We were told that all children with Down's Syndrome would have their throats x-rayed prior to surgery at the Freeman after Peter's experience.

For the rest of the Friday and the whole of Saturday, we followed a strange twilight existence, visiting Peter unbeknown to him, taking walks, eating in the hospital cafeteria and retiring to our little room high up in the modern accommodation block. The intensive care was very quiet at the weekend, and we got to know some of the nurses and to admire their dedication and considerable skills in such a life-and-death situation. We had focused the impression that Peter might stay on the ventilator over the week-end, but we had the lovely surprise on the Sunday morning to find him coming round. I shall never forget the smile he gave me when he first recognised me; he didn't smile again for a couple of days.

When we left intensive care, Peter was put in a main ward for observation while I went into a mum's room and Andy returned to Durham. I think Peter enjoyed the bustle of a bigger unit. The last couple of days, he and I returned to another mother and baby room so that we had four beds, each in ten days!

We were allowed to go home on the Thursday, slightly earlier than was expected as it was felt that Peter would recover more quickly in a familiar environment. Indeed one of the registrars had asked me whether we sedated Peter in order to cope with his hyperactivity! Certainly it has always been easier to be in our own surroundings with Peter although it was to the credit of the Freeman hospital that we left with some regret, promising to return when we visited the out-patients department. Philip, too, had come home earlier than intended so that he could collect his brother from the hospital. He had found it difficult to be away from us when he knew his brother was facing a serious operation, and he was so pleased to see him on his way to recovery. As we arrived back at 32 South Street, I knew what it meant to shed tears of joy. We were home. The operation was a success.

There would be a month of convalescence before Peter could return to school. That would not necessarily be easy, but the worst was over.

Once again Peter had brought us experiences which we would not have chosen, but which heightened our awareness of suffering. Two babies died during those ten days and the grief of the parents was heart-rending.

We also appreciated at first hand the skill and kindness of the medical staff and could not fault the treatment we received. Peter was given every consideration. To have been allowed to bring his music in to the ward was a great solace to him, and often the staff would comment on it or even sing along. His favourite tape started with 'Sally's galoshes go splishes and sploshes.' When one of the nurses told a consultant that she had been listening to 'Sally's galoshes' that morning, he wanted to know if it was the latest pop group! We found the Freeman hospital a delightful combination of relaxed friendliness and professionalism.

Today we go back to my hospital. We sit in an area I haven't seen before. I see some nurses. I go up to them. They do not take any notice of me. Perhaps if I stand longer, they will say 'hello'.

Mummy comes and takes me to see the Doctor. He looks at my chest. He seems pleased . . .

I know this part of the hospital. It is my ward. I go into the big room. I can't understand. There is somebody in my bed. I will go to the room I shared with Mummy. It looks the same. The nurses come to talk to me. 'Hello, Peter, you do look well.' I like seeing them. I come out into the corridor and sit down on the floor. I think I would like to stay.

When we returned after a month, for a check-up, we had to see the surgeon in the adult out-patients department, which Peter had not previously visited. He identified those who were nurses and went up to them, clearly expecting that they would want to talk to him, but they just got on with their tasks. There were no such problems when we went in to say 'hello' to everyone on the ward. They gave Peter a great welcome and we were amazed how much Peter remembered about where he had stayed. Clearly he didn't have bad associations—I felt he would have been perfectly happy to have become an in-patient again. As far as he was concerned, people in uniform were his friends and interested in him. We were later told by his teacher that when a physiotherapist visited his class in her white coat, Peter lifted up his jumper and vest to show her his scar, thinking she would like to see it.

It was only after Peter's operation that we appreciated how much he must have needed it. His colour improved dramatically. He had been blue only during the first week of his life, but he did have rather a high colour. Now he was pink and white. He also had more energy. Previously he had often lain down on the floor for stretches of time, as if to pace himself. He became more active.

The consultant had told us of one family where the child became so restless after the operation that it had placed a strain on them all! We certainly needed energy to keep up with Peter, but we were delighted with the results. The greatest bonus was that he seemed happier and also was enjoying life more. It had been worth going through the anxiety of such a serious operation.

Chapter 14

BOYS RUNNING

I sit in my buggy. Big boys rush in front of me. They grab one another. They collapse in a heap. The ball appears from under them. Someone picks it up and throws it. It is kicked high and hard. Everyone claps. 'Clap, Peter', says Daddy. I like it when the boys run close to me. I want to be among them.

I can't get out of my buggy. A whistle goes. At last Daddy lets me run around. A group of boys are standing nearby. There is a ball near them. I push it along the ground. One of them throws it to me. I like him. He throws it again. Daddy comes to take me home. I'm sorry. I'd like to play with the boys.

During Peter's time at home following the operation, we were very fortunate that the November weather was mild. Every Wednesday and Saturday afternoon Peter would accompany Andy to watch the school playing their rugby matches. He found this really exciting and his body would tense up when there were scrums, line-outs or any fierce activity close to him. He would love to have run into the midst of the game, probably to watch more closely, rather than to participate, and so he had to be contained in the buggy.

Peter has enjoyed all sport. Philip's cub football matches were equally attractive to him. He loves too to watch the balls being potted on our little snooker table, and to use the cue himself—with help! Cricket initially he found rather slow, and again he would try to trot on to the pitch. Now he will watch for up to two hours, particularly enjoying the fast bowling and again his body tenses in anticipation of the ball being released.

For a time sport on television absorbed him. Now he will tolerate football, rugby and American football, but it does not hold him as it did in the past.

I sit by the television. The two men fight with one another. Bump. One lands on his back. The crowd roars. He struggles in the other man's grip. He stamps his feet. He cannot get up. Then he twists. He sits on top of the other man. Once more the crowd clap. Then music plays. Words come up on the screen. Different pictures. Where are the men? I bang the television. My daddy pulls me away. I kick my feet. I want to see the men again . . .

There was a long period of time when wrestling featured on Independent Television every Saturday afternoon. This was the highlight of Peter's week. He sat on the floor, close to the screen, enthralled by the movements in front of his eyes. There were considerable problems when the adverts came on half way through, as Peter was furious to have his viewing interrupted and we would often have to act fast to prevent the television from being damaged! At the end of the programme, we would whisk Peter away to the kitchen to have his tea, before he could once again vent his anger. Wrestling certainly provided him with intense enjoyment, but I'm glad its attractions have faded!

85

Philip runs up and bowls. My daddy hits the ball with a loud crack. Mummy runs after it. I go up to my brother. 'Let Peter have a bowl.' Philip puts the ball in my hand. 'Run, run, run, bowl.' Philip propels me forward and guides my arm above my head. I throw the ball. Daddy runs forward and hits it. I run off. I'm pleased I've bowled well. Now I stand near Daddy. 'Do you want a bat, Peter?' Daddy holds my hands round the handle. Philip bowls. We hit the ball. It makes a lovely noise. I drop the bat. I move away to watch the game . . .

Peter enjoys participating in sport in short bursts, and is pleased with his achievement. He does not appreciate the competitive element, but gains satisfaction from the sound of ball on bat, or making contact with a football. He sometimes has his own logic! We have tried to interest him in skittles and placed large plastic coloured ones at the end of the room and given him the ball to bowl. To please us, he will co-operate for a little while, but at the first opportunity, he will knock them over with his hands. This shows how his mind works.

His greatest love has been swimming and he has gone there regularly with his school. He has had various buoyancy aids, a ring, arm bands and now has a suit with pockets for floats. He is being taught the appropriate movements and we are hopeful that, one day, he will swim. Water gives him enormous pleasure, and a daily bath with lots of bubbles is a necessity in Peter's life . . . unlike most boys of his age! When there has been water play at school, he has been known to get in fully clothed! Snow, however, was another matter. In Durham, we lived near a superb hill and tobogganists and even skiers would congregate on it. It was Philip's delight. Andy would take Peter down the smaller slope on a sledge a couple of times, but he ended up thoroughly miserable and rather cold. He now goes horse-riding for the disabled, but it took a long time for him to tolerate a riding-hat.

'Good boy. You walk now.' I get out of my buggy and on to the pavement. There is a gate to examine. I look closely at the pattern. I touch it. 'Come on Peter, hold my hand.' We pause at the red post box. Mummy gives me a letter and lifts me up. I post the letter. 'Come on Peter, let's run . . . Ready, steady, go'. I like the way Mummy says 'go' and then makes her feet go fast. Mine go fast too. It makes me laugh. I stop so that Mummy will say 'Ready, steady, go' again — and again.

Now I am tired. I sit down on the ground. Hands lift me from behind. I take a few steps. I see a puddle. If I bang my foot in it, I can make a lovely splash. Mummy hurries me on. Mummy sees some friends in their garden. I climb into my buggy.

Peter's liking for his own physical activity is rather variable. Nowhere has this been more true than in walking. His toddler gait also poses him problems in walking over a distance. He still cannot run or jump, and for some reason tends to go on tip-toe. Very gradually his walking is improving, but it has been a slow business and until recently we have had to take his buggy as one would with a small child. Perhaps one day Peter will be able to tramp the countryside with us.

Nonetheless sport and physical activity give Peter

enormous pleasure even if it mainly involves watching others. Each winter Saturday afternoon he and his father go and watch the school hockey and rugby matches with great enjoyment.

Chapter 15

MY GLASSES, HEARING-AID AND SPECIAL BREAD

Children with a mental handicap unfortunately often have additional medical problems, and Peter seems to have had more than his fair share of them. These in their turn, can further retard development. In addition to the infant spasms and heart defect, we soon realised that throughout his early years, Peter was very much in a world of his own. He peered very closely at everything and was not developing any speech.

We asked for his sight and his hearing to be checked again. In each instance we were referred to a specialist. The eye consultant confirmed that he needed glasses. He would have been content to have delayed prescribing them until Peter went to school, but I felt Peter required as much help as possible, being so short-sighted. The testing of sight was clearly a problem and in order to get an accurate diagnosis Peter's pupils were dilated, and he was put under general anaesthetic for his lenses to be measured. We found these days very trying—they occurred at roughly nine month intervals after this, to take into account the growth of his eyes. We feared the risks of the anaesthetic although it was a light one.

I remember before the first occasion, talking to our GP about my concern. He asked me if I regarded Peter's visual limitation as a real impediment to his progress, and, when I answered that I did, he then asked me if I believed it essential for his well-being for him to have the test. He did not minimise the anxiety but focused on the positive benefit I was seeking for Peter.

We were also worried about keeping Peter happy, when his routine and environment were so drastically changed. We used to follow an almost military procedure before our departure to the hospital, dressing Peter in his bedroom and taking him straight out to the car, so that he did not have to see any food, as, of course, he couldn't have breakfast. He spent the time waiting to be called to the theatre as a day patient in the children's ward. To begin with he was at the bottom of the list and there was even one occasion when the lunches were served before he was called! After we had told the specialist of the problems of keeping Peter content for such a long stretch of time without food, he agreed to see him earlier in the morning.

We have found that professionals have been very ready to accommodate to Peter's needs, but often we have had to point them out, especially if they have been little involved in the field of mental handicap. The eye consultant also gave Peter a regular appointment at 8.55am for his periodic visits, once he realised the difficulty of keeping him happy in a busy waiting area.

Today we go into a shop. It is full of spectacles. A tall man stands in front of me. 'Here are your glasses, Peter.' They feel heavy behind my ears, on my nose. Everything has clearer lines. I am like Daddy. The world seems too harsh, I feel confused. I throw them to the ground . . .

Initially there were problems persuading Peter to wear the glasses, but by putting them on him regularly, he eventually accepted them to the extent that he actually came to resent them being removed in the opticians to be adjusted! In fact as he grew bigger, Andy and I both had to go with him to hold his hands and feet while his glasses were taken on and off to prevent him kicking and struggling! His glasses had become so much part of his own personality.

On three occasions in his first five years we had his hearing tested, but we were told that his lack of speech was the result of the severity of his mental handicap. Again he was difficult to test and, on the third occasion, we were told that he could have his auditory responses tested under anaesthetic, but as the heart surgery, already described, was getting closer, we felt we could only take one thing at a time. We did feel concerned about Peter's lack of communication and sometimes I had dreams in which Peter talked to us!

Granny is with us. I like to ride on a train. Mummy puts a book on the table. It is my favourite, Rupert Bear. I look out of the window. We race past fields, houses, towns. Granny talks to me. I like that. Mummy is getting something else out of the bag; it is my picnic box. I love a picnic . . . Now we have left the fields behind, there are rows and rows of houses. I have never seen so many. At last we stop in an enormous station. Mummy takes me and the buggy. Granny brings the bags. Mummy lifts me down from the train. I can see more trains. There are so many people, standing, walking, running. I am pushed into the street. The buildings are tall. People rush past us. Cars and buses drive by, one after the other. I like the bustle and excitement.

There is so much to see . . . We go into one of the tall buildings. There are nurses. It is another hospital. A nurse comes and talks to Mummy. She looks at my chest. She seems pleased. Now we can go and play.

There is a toy-room. A lady gives me a musical box . . .

Once Peter's heart operation was behind us, our doctor asked if we had any more worries concerning Peter. I said that I would like now to establish finally whether he could hear properly. He referred us to The Nuffield Centre at the National Ear Nose & Throat Hospital in London and, after nearly a year, we received an appointment. We would spend two nights on the children's ward and, on the middle day, Peter would both be observed and also tested under anaesthetic. Since the date coincided with Andy's start of term, he was unable to accompany us, and so my mother offered to come along to help on the long journey and during the visit. It would have been very difficult to have managed without her assistance.

I was very impressed with 'the Nuffield'. I was asked lots of questions about Peter's responses to sound. I felt that he heard a certain amount on his left side as he held musical toys to that ear and also cupped his hand over it. Peter was observed from behind a glass panel, by a team of specialists as he played and his reaction to a variety of sounds was noted. Finally he was put under anaesthetic and his auditory responses were tested. In this instance he was very distressed as he came round, and it took four of us to hold him as he thrashed around. Eventually he calmed down. We finally learnt what we had long suspected, that Peter was virtually deaf on the right hand side, and had partial hearing on the left. He could wear a hearing-aid in that ear.

I am happy to be out in the streets again. We stop outside a shop. Granny goes in. When she comes out, she is carrying a large parcel. We move on. We see some green grass. We sit on a bench. Granny unwraps the parcel. It is full of fish and chips. I like them. We often eat them, on holiday. Mummy holds them in front of me. I am hungry. I eat quickly. Mummy and Granny are hungry too . . .

We leave the park and go back into the busy roads. There is our car. I would like a ride. I wriggle in my buggy. Mummy unfastens the strap. I try to open the door. Mummy grabs me. 'No, Peter, that isn't our car.' I want to get in the car. I want to drive home. I struggle. I am sure it's our car. Mummy picks me up. I am cross. She pushes me back into my buggy.

I try to stop her. I struggle. I kick. She is stronger than me. She fastens my strap and pushes me away from the car. I am angry and sad. I cry.

Following the long morning of tests on our second day in London, we were allowed to take Peter out of the hospital, but we were not allowed to go home until the following day to ensure that he had fully recovered from the anaesthetic. One might imagine that a child with Down's Syndrome would be confused by the busy London streets, Peter seemed to love the hurly-burly of it.

On this outing our only difficult moment came when we passed a Renault 5 parked by the kerb. Peter indicated he wanted to get out of his buggy. Optimistically and mistakenly, I thought he wanted to walk, but to my cost found that he expected to be able to ride away in a car, identical to ours. It was very hard work to get him back into his buggy as he developed a full-scale tantrum when he was thwarted. A gentleman passing by gave me a very dubious look as I forcibly placed a furious Peter back into his buggy!

Apart from that episode, and Peter's distress following the anaesthetic, the visit to London went far better than I had dared to hope. A month later, Andy and I took Peter on a day return to London to have his hearing-aid fitted. We were shown how to place the mould in his left ear and hook the aid behind it. It was suggested that we should get him to wear it for short periods of time in the house. Mrs Watson also helped by putting it in at school, and we reached the stage where Peter was wearing it for half an hour or so, at a time, and even going out for rides in his buggy with it in his ear. At first we had had to hold his hands to prevent him from removing it, but he seemed to be accepting it.

Unfortunately progress with the hearing aid did not continue smoothly. Since our move to Suffolk followed shortly after, and Peter took a long time to settle into a new school, it was out of the question for him to wear it there. He continued to wear it for short periods but only at home. Then after about a year, he had to have a new mould made, to take into account the growth of his ear. This seemed a more cumbersome object and Peter certainly knew the difference. He disliked it intensely and at the sight of it became angry and upset. We had another new mould made, but the damage had been done. Finally, on a visit to the Nuffield, when he was nine and a half, following a very happy journey and play in the waiting area, Peter became very distressed as soon as he entered the doctor's consulting room. He did not wish to have his ears examined, nor did he wish to have his hearing-aid put in. We talked about having a more expensive and sensitive aid, which might be less disturbing for Peter, for, of course, he was unable to tell us whether we had fixed the volume at the right level. In the end we were recommended to abandon the hearing-aid altogether, as it was causing stress to Peter and anxiety to ourselves, and to compensate for the hearing loss by speaking to Peter on the left side. Reluctantly we agreed that this was the best thing to do.

Whether Peter would have accepted an aid had we been able to obtain a satisfactory diagnosis of his hearing loss at an early age is the unanswerable question. Nowadays the fact that many children with Down's Syndrome suffer a hearing loss is more widely accepted than it was a decade ago and there is a greater awareness of the problem. Peter has always enjoyed sounds, as his love of music indicates, so we could now best help him by raising the volume of his cassette player as well as our voices, and using gesture and facial expression to reinforce what we are saying.

My tummy is always aching. The pains move up and down, in waves. Once again Mummy takes me upstairs to the bathroom. She runs the water and undresses me. She puts me in the bath. I don't like her letting the water out. She turns the taps on again. This time she pours in bubbles. I like that. I can touch them, pat them, watch the colours dance in them . . .

When Peter was six, his tummy was often very upset. We seemed to be cleaning him up several times a day. We had a specimen tested to see if he had an infection and the results were negative. The doctor then asked us if there had been any change in his diet. Peter had been eating with great relish a lot of bread and butter, and Weetabix. They seemed to be particular favourites. We were then told to eliminate wheat from his diet to see if it was causing the problem. The results were dramatic. His tummy upsets ceased from then on. We had to get special gluten-free bread, flour and biscuits from the chemist on prescription. I tried rye bread and oatcakes but found that they also affected him adversely. Fortunately Peter enjoys meat and vegetables and does not have a particularly sweet tooth and he does not seem to mind the rather tasteless gluten-free bread, although we have to keep the ordinary bread-bin well out of his reach, as he will eat ours in preference. Accommodating his diet is now part of our way of life. A great bonus resulting from the elimination of gluten was that Peter became happier in himself. His discomfort must have been considerable.

Peter is diagnosed as a multi-handicapped child by the medical profession as a result of the variety of his disabilities. These disabilities help to account for the degree of his retardation. Nonetheless by trying to overcome them or compensate for them, we can still enable him to enjoy his life as much as possible.

Chapter 16

OUR MOVE

There is a big case beside me. Something under my feet. The car starts. We go through miles and miles of open country. The engine hums. I like it when we go fast. We don't go very fast today. Eventually we stop. Daddy opens my picnic box. I eat my cold meat and beetroot, crisps and mousse. Still we drive on. I look at my book. I like the little figures on the page. It begins to get dark. I can't see any more. Mummy and Daddy sound anxious. At last we stop. We go into a big bungalow. Mummy puts on my music in the kitchen. She bustles around getting tea. I am hungry. We have sausage and chips, ice-cream, and bread and butter. That was nice. Now I can go home. I pick up my coat from the chair and try to open the door. 'No, Peter,' says Mummy 'we are going to live here now.' What does she mean?

Andy was due to start his new job as deputy head of a co-educational boarding-school in Suffolk in January 1985. After twelve years we were to leave Durham which had been the only home the boys had ever known. Philip felt very sad. It was impossible to explain to Peter all that was going to happen. It was outside his experience.

Before Christmas, Andy and I moved all our furniture and belongings, while Peter stayed at Sister Mac's, and Philip in Goathland. We then returned north to have Christmas in our bungalow in Yorkshire, and all moved south a couple of days later. Peter clearly did not regard his new home as permanent on the first day, but he never again fetched his coat to leave. Perhaps the familiar furniture convinced him that we were here to stay. He seemed to enjoy the space and wandering from room to room in our new bungalow. We were relieved we did not have to worry about him going upstairs and the dangers of his falling out of a window! We explored the extensive school grounds and appreciated being able to push the buggy on flat ground after the steepness of Durham.

We come to a front door. Daddy rings the bell. A lady says brightly 'Do come in.' Mummy sits me beside her and gives me a book. I look at a picture then throw it on the floor. I want to explore.

Flames are dancing. Can I get close? Mummy follows me. She holds me tight. She gives me my musical radio. More people come into the room. They all say 'Hello, Peter.' We go into another room for tea. There is ham on my plate. I have some crisps, some bread. Everyone else eats cakes. Why can't I have them? I try and get down. 'Sit still' says Mummy, but the lady says I can go. I walk into the hall. I cry. I want to go home. A nice girl talks to me. She wants to see my toys . . .

During the ten days or so before term started it seemed as if we were in some kind of limbo, in a rural flat land, so different from Durham, hardly knowing anyone. Gradually we met new folk and twice we were invited out. I really wondered how we and Peter would cope, remembering times when he had, in the past, set up a howl on the door-step of a strange home. Happily, he trotted into these strange houses without a qualm, and, although he needed very close supervision to ensure his own safety, as well as making sure he did not damage anything, he managed well. Outwardly he seemed to be adjusting happily to the radical changes that were occurring in his life, but we just did not anticipate how traumatic he was going to find the next upheaval — a new school.

I had taken the Open University post-experience course 'the handicapped person in the community', a couple of years previously and in one unit there was an example to illustrate the difficulty experienced by mentally handicapped people in coping with change. A boy in his teens had lived in a very friendly street and had been used to calling in on his neighbours, sure of a welcome. When he moved, he could not understand why he didn't get the same reception. He became very unhappy. As I read this sad story, I had thought that it would not apply if *we* moved, as Peter was not accustomed to making visits on his own. I should have appreciated the wider implications. In Peter's case it was a new school that posed the problem for him.

Chapter 17

MY NEW SCHOOL

We stop by a school building. Mummy takes my hand. We go through the front door and into a classroom. The teacher lets me look at a toy, while she talks to Mummy. Then Mummy says 'goodbye'. The teacher talks to me. I don't understand all she says. I think I'd better sit at the table. She gives me a paper and pencil. I throw them on the floor. What am I doing here? I am confused. Where is Mrs Watson? Why can't I play? I push the little girl next to me. She cries. I sit on the floor. My sadness overwhelms me. I bang my head again and again . . . Later we go into the hall. We pass bigger children. No one says 'Hello, Peter Morgan.'

The change of school proved to be a very difficult experience for Peter. From the age of three, he had been in the same nursery class. He had only known two teachers. The atmosphere had been informal. In Suffolk, he was initially placed in a class for 8—10 year-olds, as it was about the time of his eighth birthday. Despite several requests, the education department had not allowed his papers to be released until we had moved, and his new school did not have his records. I had noted on my first visit that the school had high expectations and that quite a lot of formal work was done in the mornings. I cherished hopeful and totally unrealistic thoughts that Peter might make progress by leaps and bounds and even begin to read! Instead, he developed real behavioural problems. He head-banged, became aggressive to other children and had severe temper tantrums. He was disrupting the life of the school. He had expressed his frustrations forcibly before, but somehow this was more concentrated and more worrying. We received a 'phone call from the headmaster after a few days saying that he was going to be moved into a special care class. Special care! In Durham, that had meant children with severe physical as well as mental handicaps. How did Peter fit into that category? Yet clearly the class in which he had been originally placed was inappropriate.

Later in the term I was called in to meet the psychiatrist who was seeing Peter. Whereas in Durham the psychiatrist saw all mentally handicapped children, in Suffolk they were the concern of the paediatrician unless there were problems, when a psychiatrist was called in. I met the new teacher, Mrs Mace, and began to feel happier. I was sure that she would do all she could to help Peter. There were several children in the class similar to Peter, as well as a couple in wheel chairs. Special care seemed to mean something different here. Gradually Peter settled himself although we knew that he still had temper tantrums and aggressive outbursts.

'Hello Peter', says Mrs Mace 'shall we take off your coat?' She undoes the zip and I take it off and give it to her. Together we place it on the peg. No other children are here yet. I must wait for

Claire. I stand by the door. Here is somebody. It isn't Claire. It's Nikky. Who is this? It's Sean. Where is Claire? Is she coming now? 'Hello Claire,' says Mrs Mace 'shall we take off your coat?' I help. I am pleased to see Claire. We hang up her coat. We sit down side by side at the table. Mac gives me the trigger jigger. I place cups on the stick and press them down. I press the knob. They fly into the air. Claire is pleased . . .

'Come and help me make the coffee,' calls Mac. I trot over to the door. I like going on my own with Mac to the kitchen. She talks to me all the time and I help her put the empty cups ready. I like to watch her. She is my special friend.

Mrs Mace has arranged the chairs in a circle. I sit beside her. She begins to sing. *Old MacDonald had a farm.* She makes lots of funny noises. So does Mac. Now they sing *One evening Cousin Peter came.* They point at me. I smile. I like this song about me. I stand up. 'Sit down, Pete,' they say.

Eventually school proved to be a great success. Peter's behavioural problems receded as he became thoroughly familiar with the new routine and surroundings. Mrs Mace and her assistant, Mac, were very good to him. He also made a special friend, Claire. She is almost his age, and although she does not have Down's Syndrome, very similar. She lacks speech, but loves being talked to. Peter obviously thought her very special and both seemed to want to be near each other and to communicate in their own way. The psychiatrist was delighted with this development as it signified Peter forming a close relationship with someone of his own age and outside the family and becoming far more aware of those around him.

After five terms, a new special care class was made, called transition. Judy Mace and Mac were put in charge of it, and there are four children including Peter and Claire, who are all ambulant but have problems which prevent them from being in the mainstream classes. Peter seems very happy with the new arrangement and enjoys his many activities—his work programme, singing, cooking, soft play, his group sessions with the physiotherapist, swimming and occasional outings. When Judy moved away from the area last year and was replaced by Richard, Peter adjusted well. He goes into school with an enormous grin on his face, each morning. He has become much calmer and more settled. Life in Suffolk seems to suit Peter well.

Chapter 18

NEW FRIENDS

What activities is Peter able to undertake outside the school? To whom can he relate beyond his immediate circle? The possibilities are limited for a severely handicapped child and often opportunities have to be found or created. We wished to continue to build on Peter's love of music.

Mummy puts the chair by the piano. Margaret is coming. Here she is now. I take her hand. I pull her across the lounge and I put her hands on the keys. She puts the song book in front of her. I sit on the chair beside her. Margaret plays about Cousin Peter. At the end, she runs her thumb down

the keys and bongs me on the nose. I laugh. I sit
on her knee. I put my hands on the back of hers.
Our hands race up and down. I don't like the next
tune. I turn the page . . .

It took us almost two years to find a successor to
Dr Urquhart. Now Margaret Nunn comes to our house
once a fortnight for half an hour. For about half the time
Peter is closely involved in what she is doing. Then he
usually retires to sit by his toy cupboard, but we can tell
that he is still in fact listening to every note and responding
to the music.

My minibus is here. Mummy takes my hand. We
walk over to it. I am helped up the steps. I go to
my usual seat. We follow the normal route. We
pick up a boy in the next village. Then we go to
the school where some of the children get out. I
stay still. We go to my school next, but no, we turn
up the lane to Family Help. I must be going to
see Mrs Cresswell and the other children. I am
pleased, I like it here. I see my friends. Everyone
talks to me. I can play in the garden. I stand up
ready to get out. 'Sit down, Peter', says Kate.
'We are collecting John.' I sit down on the cloor.
I cry and cry.

Very soon after our move to Suffolk I made contact
with the Social Services, as I knew there would be times
when I would need to leave Peter in someone else's care,

and we had no friends or relatives nearby. We were put into contact with the Family Help Unit, run by the Spastic Society, in which Suffolk was taking up a number of places for short-term care. Peter first of all went for a day and then overnight, until he was able to stay for nine nights recently. On several occasions, he gave us clear evidence that he really enjoyed his visits. Once when I was driving in the locality, Peter became very angry with me when I did not turn down Shakers Lane. Similarly the driver of the school minibus was faced with a very irate Peter, when she collected someone else from the Unit and he was not allowed to get out.

Peter has kept one link with his past. He has occasionally visited Sister Mac, as we kept our bungalow for two years after our move and then bought a house in Scarborough. We never dared to take him back to Durham in case it would confuse him. He might expect to return to our old home and be upset because he could not go in.

Russell grabs me and gives me a hug. 'Peter', he says. I can see more of my friends. There is Martin playing football in the hall. Wendy asks me if I'd like to play Pool. She puts the balls on the table. She helps me hold the cue. We tap the ball sharply, it runs into the others. They scatter in all directions . . . Mrs Ashman takes me to a table. She has a big mixing bowl. I stir the cake . . . Someone is laying the table. We are going to have our dinner soon. I sit down. I like my dinners here.

A few months after our move I heard about the Jubilee Club for mentally handicapped children, once a month on a Saturday run by the Red Cross. In September 1986, I decided to ask if Peter could become a member. The meetings are held in a youth club which happens to be adjacent to the car park for the Leisure Centre. On the first occasion, Peter thought he should go swimming and protested vigorously as I took him into the Rendez-vous. I had a sinking feeling inside, fearing Peter was going to make an unfavourable impression. I stayed with him while he settled down.

The special activity for that day was in fact to go swimming! We returned from the pool for a hot meal. Then I left Peter to have a play for an hour so that he didn't expect me to be always with him at the club. The next month, he waved when I took his coat off, and so I realised this was *his* outing. I was delighted. The club is run by several parents who bring along their normal young children. Some teenagers and young adults also assist. Peter has the opportunity to make new friends on his own. Recently he has joined the Breakaway Club run by some older teenagers fortnightly on a Sunday afternoon.

'I am pleased you have come to see me, Peter.' Mrs Davies gives me a nice welcome. We take off my coat. I go into the sitting room. The Jack-in-the-box is on the table. I wind it. Jack pops up. Mummy gives me my musical radio and my books. I flop down on the big cushions by the window. The other children like my books. Mummy is talking and drinking coffee. I wonder when we are going to eat. I get up and go out into the dining room. Why isn't the table laid? Where is my place?

104

Mrs Davies comes in. 'Sorry Peter, it isn't dinner time.'

I go into the hall and pick up my coat. Mummy takes it from me. 'No! Peter, you come in the sitting room and have some crisps . . .'

Peter has made several friends in our neighbourhood. He used to enjoy the girls from the school, baby-sitting. He especially likes his visit to the Davies' household. We go periodically for Sunday lunch, which is much appreciated by Peter. When we have visited at other times, he hasn't been able to understand why he is not invited to sit up to the usual delicious meal, and he has amused us by getting his coat when he has found that food is not on the agenda!

We go into a hall. People sit in rows. We sit behind them. I am in my buggy. Daddy and Mummy are beside me. Someone talks at the front. I do not understand. Music starts up. I like that. People are singing. It stops. More people talk. I take Daddy's hand and place it on the handle of my buggy. I'd like to go home. Mummy gives me a book. I push it away. I start to complain. I take Daddy's hand again. He gets up and pushes me outside . . .

In Durham Peter had been able to make friends in the church and attend part of the worship. The Anglican Services we first attended in Suffolk were far more formal and peaceful. The congregation was welcoming, but

eventually we realised that we needed to worship somewhere where Peter's noises were less obtrusive. We had
made some friends in a new Fellowship of Christians
meeting in a community centre. They were keen to include
Peter, but he would agitate to leave almost as soon as the
Service started! The lights, music, stained glass windows
and atmosphere of a traditional church are clearly special
to him, so, although we could join in some activities together, it was difficult for us to worship as a family there.
Then we found that Peter did enjoy the services in a
nearby village church. The small congregation is very
friendly and we are able to worship as a family on most
Sundays.

Peter also enjoys having visitors to our house. Cynthia,
who used to come down from the school to help me about
four hours each week, was his greatest friend and fan. He
liked to sit near her while she worked.

'You must sit still Peter. Ann cannot cut your
hair if you wriggle.' I don't want my hair cut. It is
mine. I am upset. I cry. Daddy holds me firmly on
his knee. Mummy puts on my favourite tunes. Ann
goes snip, snip, round my ears. It tickles on the
back of my neck. 'Look up, Peter.' I don't want to
look up. I struggle to get free. Daddy holds me
more firmly still. Hairs land on my nose. I don't
like it. I cry. 'That will be fine, Ann. Thank you,'
says Mummy.

While they say goodbye to Ann, I sit on the
kitchen floor and try to put my hair back on.

One visitor about whom Peter had some initial reservations was Ann. She used to come once a month to cut everyone's hair. At first Peter was difficult. Clearly he regarded having his hair cut as removing something very personal to himself. Ann was very patient and gradually he accepted the necessity. When Ann stopped working in this area, Peter had to get used to Michael, who was always happy to give him a lot of his time. Now he is able to cut his hair with only one or two minor protests. Peter grins as we all tell him how smart he looks.

It can take Peter a while to accept new situations but we hope that we can widen his horizons gradually, so that he can lead a varied and satisfying life.

Chapter 19

AT HOME

We feel that home is very important to Peter. It gives him a secure base. When he has been away for a short break, he seems to revel in the rediscovery of his favourite toys and books. He settles down in his favourite places, sits on his chair by the kitchen table, flops on the Rupert Bear bean bag in his bedroom, puts his books on the coffee table and sits down with his legs stretched out underneath, finds the pool of sunlight by the front door or the french windows.

'We've got presents for you, Peter' says Philip. He thrusts a packet into my hands. Mummy helps me open it. It is a T-shirt. 'Here's something else.' They unwrap a small parcel for me. It is a tape.

They put it on. The music is strange. 'Come on, let's dance.' We all stand in a circle. We hold hands. We skip and move in time to the music. They are so pleased with me. I can feel their happiness. I want to show mine. They often kiss me. Now I kiss them, lots of times on their hands.

In addition to familiarity of place, we like to think that we all matter a great deal to Peter. He gave us the best indication of this, when Andy, Philip and I returned from a week's holiday in Crete, when he was nine. Normally he enjoys being cuddled and will from time to time come and sit on our knees, but he isn't particularly demonstrative himself. However that summer was the exception. He seemed to want to show both his feelings for us and his pleasure at our return, to the best of his ability. We had heard that he had been content going to school from the Family Help Unit, and so it wasn't a reaction to being miserable. In fact I had probably been much more upset about leaving him than he was at being left. To receive such a tremendous welcome home was a real bonus.

Mummy runs the bath water. It seems too early. 'Want to make you a smart boy,' she says. I help her undress me. I make sure she puts the bubbles in. I put my toe carefully in the water. It feels right. I get in. I try to catch the bubbles. I splash vigorously. Mummy comes in. 'No, Peter, you are swamping the floor. I'll have to get you out.' We go into my bedroom. She dries me. I examine the Mister Men on the curtains. I put on clean clothes. Usually I put on my pyjamas after my bath. We go into the sitting room. The table is laid. A car draws up. A lady and gentleman get out with Daddy. Now I can sit up at the table. The others join me. I am happy we have visitors. I want Daddy to blow kisses on my hand. He says 'excuse me' to the visitors. I like a special meal. I have three helpings of ice-cream. After the supper the grown-ups have coffee. I am too excited to sit down. 'Sit still' says Mummy. I can't . . . Quite soon, the visitors go. Mummy and Daddy wash up and then Daddy takes me to my bedroom to put on my pyjamas. He does my teeth, says 'good-night' and shuts the door. He can't do that. I haven't had my drink in the kitchen. How can he forget? The anger overwhelms me. I bang my head on the door. Daddy and Mummy rush in. They must have forgotten. My tears subside. I sit at the kitchen table and have my drink. Then I will go to bed.

As well as appreciating familiar places and people, Peter is also a stickler for routine. We have obviously been affected by this, although we have tried not to become hide-bound. Our days do have a pattern, although we aim not to make it too rigid. Each weekday morning, Andy will dress Peter with his help, while I get the breakfast. Peter always sits at the same place at meals, that is beside his father who supervises him while I get the food on the table. He eats with a fork or a dessert spoon and gets very upset if we put a dessert spoon with a patterned handle in front of him. He likes his to be plain. He loves examining the jam and marmalade pots and cereal packets.

After breakfast he plays a little and waits for his mini-bus to take him to school. Sometimes he collects his coat from the cupboard. When he returns from school, the first task is to put him on the toilet as it will be an hour since this has happened. In order to keep him dry, we have to take him regularly, as he rarely indicates that he needs to go.

We started the toilet training at the age of two. Had I been told then that would continue until he was twelve, I think I would have been very demoralised! It was a landmark when recently we were able to give up the use of pads altogether. The next sign of real progress will be for Peter to indicate his need for the toilet.

At about four o'clock, Peter expects a substantial snack as he has had a packed lunch on account of his gluten-free diet. We therefore sit down together, with Philip sometimes joining us on his return from school. After tea, Peter plays, listens to his music, looks at his books. In the summer, we may take him for a walk. He enjoys watching me prepare food and will stir a cake. He now understands it takes time for me to prepare a meal. He used to expect instant service! About six o'clock we all eat together and Peter will have a bath after this. Between eight and eight-thirty, he will go to his room, listen to his music and look at his books again. After an hour we will take him to the toilet again, then tuck him up. We may well have to repeat this after another hour as he is frequently still awake at ten-thirty. He has to be woken at seven-thirty in the morning. Usually he will be dry. In the holidays and at weekends, the routine can be no less rigid.

How does Peter relate to each of us in the family? I always feel that Andy is perhaps his greatest friend. He has been closely involved with caring for him since babyhood. I am sure his strong arms are very reassuring for Peter. They play rough and tumble games together and enjoy each other's company. Peter and I are more quietly companionable! In term time we spend most time together, as Andy and Philip are often busy after four o'clock, and, of course, there are Saturday morning classes for them, and, often, other school activities arranged for the weekend.

As for Philip it has not always been easy for him, particularly when Peter was younger and related more to Andy and myself than anyone else, as a small baby might. Philip could then feel excluded by Peter. There was also a time when he would nip Philip and enjoy the ensuing furore he caused, which was upsetting. Philip has always loved Peter which made any rough treatment harder to bear. Happily Peter has calmed down and that phase has more or less passed. He shows great pleasure at his brothers's company.

Several years ago, Philip had to write an essay on an interesting member of his family saying why he or she is special. Extracts from the composition will indicate better than I can the way in which they relate to one another:-

Having discussed his medical condition Philip went on to say:—

. . . 'Peter has taught himself his own sign language. He will give his plate to ask for something to eat. If he wants to go out he will get his coat, etc.

'I cannot remember what I felt when I knew Peter was handicapped. I think I just grew up with it . . .

'Peter's favourite hobbies are reading books (he frequently raids my bookshelf), listening to music and riding in cars. He spends most of the day reading or running up and down the hall. I don't know if he actively reads the books or just looks at them.

'I often wonder what Peter thinks of me. I think he recognises me as his brother. He likes to play funny games with me. He grabs my nose and pulls it left and right and I have to say 'dong, dong, dong'. Another favourite game is to put his hand against my mouth so I can blow a raspberry on his hand and that can be embarrassing.

'Peter is very energetic and runs around on tiptoe, but he does not often like to walk. He prefers to sit in his buggy and be pushed. He is very sweet, but

111

often hits and pinches people to show his excitement. I think I prefer having him to a normal brother.'

In addition to home, Andy's school is also part of the familiar environment which Peter enjoys.

My daddy pushes me up the path, through the woods. We go towards the houses where the boys and girls live. 'Hello Mr Morgan, hello Pete. How are you?' Tanya stops for a chat. Next we meet the nice man who always makes a special fuss of me. 'Come on Pete, out of the buggy. You can have a ride. Come on sit on my knee. Press the horn.' He takes my hand and presses a knob. A loud peep sounds. He helps me to do it again. We ride around on the grass. The other boys watch. They too want a ride. At last we stop. 'That's enough for today, Pete.' Daddy takes my hand and says thank you for me. We walk along the path and down the steps. I'd like to go in the boys' houses. I go to the door. 'Not today' says Daddy. I sit down. Perhaps he will change his mind. He picks me up, puts me in the buggy. He says we have to go home for dinner.

A boarding school is a very good place for Peter to live. When we walk out into the grounds, we see other people moving about the place. Some talk to him, particularly the girls who baby-sat, and the staff who live on the site. The junior boys' housemaster has made a mechanised trike and sometimes takes Peter for rides.

Peter especially enjoys the sport, and also the times

when he is allowed to go into the main old house with its potential for echoes. He again may meet people who will greet him. He may not be able to talk, but he loves to be spoken to and certainly doesn't appreciate being ignored!

Chapter 20

A BIRTHDAY PARTY

I half open my eyes. I tell myself I'll read my favourite book when Philip bursts in. 'Happy Birthday, Pete.' He takes my hand. 'Come and see Mummy and Daddy.'

'Happy Birthday, Peter,' 'Happy Birthday, Peter.' My daddy lifts me up and cuddles me and rolls me over to the middle of the bed. I like the welcome. Philip has a stack of parcels in his arms. 'Your presents, Pete.' I know about presents. We had them at Christmas. I pull at the brightly coloured wrapping paper and inside there is some-times something I like. Inside one packet is a jumper. Everyone seems very excited. 'You will look smart, Pete,' they tell me. I like the funny shaped parcel. Inside one half is a green cup and plate. Mummy is pleased about that. The other half has two Annuals; lots of lovely little pictures to look at. I begin to read. My brother wants to read too. I have to keep taking a book back from him. Mummy puts parcels under my nose. I prefer my new books. Mummy keeps saying 'Open this one, Peter'. In the end I pull at the paper. Inside are some keys like our piano. 'A keyboard from Uncle Roger, you lucky boy' says Philip. 'Can I have a go?' He makes lovely sounds. They change when he slides a knob. I like knobs. I touch one, I put my fingers on the keys. I like this present . . .

My daddy and I drive out in the car. We go to my teacher's house. I have been there before. I do not go in this time, but she comes and sits beside me in the back. I am glad to see her. I wonder why she is here. She comes back to my house. Mummy is waiting . . .

Soon some children arrive. They put a parcel in my hand. I tear the paper. Some soap and bubble-bath fall out. I don't need that now; I throw it on the floor. 'Thank you Tim and Alison,' says Mummy. 'Peter will like that. He loves his bath.' Matthew arrives and I find a book in his parcel. Hannah arrives, she gives me playdoh. We all play some games. Judy takes my hand. She says we're looking for Christmas cards. There is another knock at the door. Is there someone else? It is Claire, my friend from my class. She brings her sister and mummy and daddy. I am very happy to see all these people at my house. My brother comes in and we all sit up at the table for tea. I am very hungry. There are things I like. Sausages, crisps, cake, jelly. My daddy puts food on my plate. They say I eat a lot. The lights go out. Mummy lights my candles. I love their brightness, and the way the flames dance. 'Who is going to help Peter blow them out?' Matthew puffs hard. It is darkness again. Philip puts the big lights on.

The best game after tea is balloon football. I like to burst the balloons. I like the pop. Why do they say 'keep the balloon away from Peter'? I catch it and dig my fingers in it. It jumps from my hands. The children laugh. 'It's a good job these balloons seem especially tough' says Mummy. Claire's mummy says it is time to go. I have enjoyed my party.

Celebrations are important in Peter's life. His tenth birthday party was a very happy occasion as I saw his involvement and pleasure. It enabled me to appreciate the progress he had made. Because his development is slow, it is only after an interval that I can see what he has achieved.

This was the last time we organised a children's party for Peter's birthday! He loved the tea, the musical games and the balloons, but the 'normal' children whom he would invite to join him were outgrowing these kind of parties. We also had to consider whether Peter should have a celebration more appropriate to his age.

When he was eleven, we invited his class to lunch, it being a school day. Judy, Mac and the three children enjoyed a hot meal and then Margaret came and played the piano to them all.

There are lots and lots of children in rows. They shout. I hear music. I want to get close. I lean over. Philip holds on to my trousers. Daddy sits me firmly on my seat. Huge curtains swish back. Brightly dressed ladies dance. A man in black comes. Everyone hisses. There is a flash and a puff of smoke . . . The curtains close. It is time to go home. Daddy takes me to the toilet. He wants me to return to my seat. I sit on the floor. He lifts me on to a different chair. The music strikes up. I'm happy again. Here's the boy Wishy Washee. Why does everyone shout 'Yo'?

We decided to go to the pantomime for Peter's 12th birthday. The local theatre is Georgian and so we had a box close to the stage. I really thought that Peter was going to propel himself over the top and into the pit when the two musicians began to play. Happily he did settle down to enjoy the spectacle. The interval posed a problem in that he thought the performance was over and was extremely reluctant to return to his place. We put him on a chair in the second row of the box for the rest of the production and sensed that he felt more secure. *We* did as well! We were pleased that, in the end, he enjoyed the whole three hours.

I believe Peter increasingly appreciates his own birthday, but he enjoys all celebrations. If we are having a special meal as a family, or entertaining, he will be the first in his seat, and so we have to make sure that we do not lay the table too much in advance, otherwise it will soon be in disarray. At Christmas we have to put the crackers by our places as we sit down, otherwise Peter will pull all of them by himself. He is more interested in the bang than the contents. Occasionally we have entertained twenty or thirty to a barbecue and Peter has become very excited by so much company and has tucked vigorously into the food.

Peter's evident enjoyment of special occasions, no matter whose, has enhanced the pleasure of all.

Chapter 21

I'M A BIG BOY NOW

At last the top step. I go into the living room. Margaret undoes my zip. I take off my coat. I wave to Mummy. She talks to Margaret. I sit down on the comfortable big chair. Tinkerbell sits close to me. I touch her. She twitches her tail. She looks at me. I pat her. I go into my room. Good, my case is here. I take my books off the shelf and put them on the floor. I sit down and look at them. I'd better go and see if Margaret has been cooking. I go into the kitchen . . .

In January 1988, an important change occurred in our life and especially in Peter's. He was linked with John and Margaret Smith, under the West Suffolk Hospitality scheme, whereby handicapped people are befriended by individuals, couples or families and invited regularly to their homes. We had put Peter's name down very soon after our move, but it had taken three years for the right link to materialize. John and Margaret are ideal. They both work with mentally handicapped adults as residential care officers with the Mencap Homes Foundation and so fully understand Peter's needs. Sometimes Peter will go to tea mid-week and then come home at about seven o'clock. He may stay the night occasionally or go for the day on a Saturday or Sunday. He usually visits two or three times a month. The introduction was gradual, but once established took off very quickly without any problems.

The first time Peter went to Margaret and John's first floor maisonette, having seen them at our house previously, he went in without a qualm and appeared immediately at ease. I marvelled at his self-assurance, having experienced his insecurity in strange surroundings so many times. Margaret and John give him their time and prepare delicious meals including home-made bread which needless to say he thoroughly enjoys. I did wonder how he would react to the four cats as he has always been fascinated by animals, but wary and on his guard if they came close. In fact he has made a special friend of Tinkerbell. Peter likes us to leave straight-way; we feel that he is telling us that this is the place where he is special. We are delighted that he can visit another home without us accompaying him and we feel that this gives him confidence and helps him to mature. After all his brother goes to his friends' homes and it is right that Peter can do the same. An added bonus has been his friendship with the eight residents of Margaret's group home which is nearby. They have come to see us at our bungalow. Peter enjoyed this, as did we all, for they are so open, friendly and appreciative.

Other developments have occurred as Peter has entered upon adolescence. For example, it has become apparent that we needed a sitter who could look after Peter throughout the evening, taking him to the toilet and attending to his various requirements. Over the last year and a half Selina has come to our house, perhaps two evenings a month, and has been a great help. She is about to embark on a nursing career and will be less available, and so we shall have to find someone else. Often parents of youngsters with mental handicap find they may have to go out separately because of the problems of finding a sitter and this is a matter of concern.

Peter has also become aware of the changes going on in his body, and we are having to teach him appropriate behaviour; that he cannot for instance slip his hand inside his trousers in public. Without making an issue of it, we either remove his hand, ask him to do so, or distract him, and hope that with repetition he will learn what is acceptable. In this as in other areas we are co-operating with his new teacher, Richard.

At school there is a continued emphasis on social skills to enable Peter to take his place in the community. The children visit the shops and public places and Peter is expected to walk everywhere. In this, he is more compliant with his teachers than us. We have recently abandoned his buggy which is a big step forward. We may find we have an irate Peter on our doorstep, as he realises he is expected to go for a walk, to the extent that he may throw a paddy, which these days includes scratching his neck rather than head-banging. By being firm and trying to be unruffled, we believe we are winning this battle, certainly in the town, having ridden there in the car, he is happy to walk some distance.

Obviously Peter has, at times, to fall in with the wishes of others, but he also needs to be able to express his own preferences and to find that they are met and so we are trying to ensure that he is able to make choices where appropriate, for example over leisure activities or whether he wants crisps or a sandwich, etc. It is all too easy to make decisions for handicapped people, but on reflection they should be responsible for as many aspects of their own life as possible, especially as they get older.

Peter is a determined boy with decided ideas. At school and at home we are increasingly using Makaton signs to facilitate communication. Makaton is a simplified version of the British sign language for the deaf used by mentally handicapped people along with the spoken word. Peter must now make the sign, 'please' when he wants crisps, rather than giving me a shove towards the place where they are kept! Soon we shall teach him the sign for 'crisps' as well. When we need Peter to be obedient, we warn him of what is to happen. For example at around half past eight I may point to my watch and say, 'Peter it is nearly time for bed', than I put my hands together and put them against the side of my head—the sign for bed. Richard is following a similar policy to indicate what is about to happen at school. Much of Peter's learning has to be taught, but sometimes he takes the initiative and instigates change.

The study door is open. I go to the shelf with the big books. I take one out. It does not look very interesting. I remove another one. It is lovely and fat. I take it into the kitchen. I sit at the table. I turn the pages. I'm like Mummy and Daddy and Philip. Mummy comes in. 'Oh Peter, you are a naughty boy, where did you get that?' She puts another book in front of me and takes away the one I was reading. I think I'll go to my bedroom. I grab the cassette recorder. 'Take care Pete, you've forgotten the wire' says Mummy. 'Which tape do you want, your jazz?' Mummy puts on the music. I take her hand to press a button. I don't like that tune. I want another one.

As Peter in the past of his own volition changed from small children's books to annuals by grabbing Philip's books where possible, so later he seemed determined to get hold of our Bibles, Dictionaries, Shakespeares, the *Oxford Book of English Verse,* etc. Certainly turning the pages of a thick book appears to be very satisfying for him, but we do wonder whether he also wishes to be more adult. We have had to put a bolt on the study to protect our books, as Peter's constant patting and turning of pages eventually spoils them, and also to allow him to have a few of his own. For a long time a heavy tome on geology was his favourite! His taste in music has also changed, and he is less interested in childrens songs, but now especially enjoys brass bands, music hall songs and jazz. 'Mac the knife' is his favourite tune and he will want me to 'fast forward' the tape so that he can listen to it straightaway.

Recently he has also wished to spend time in his bedroom with his music and will suddenly take off with his cassette recorder, without fully appreciating that he also needs the wire. He has some inkling that the recorder cannot work itself and one day I found him trying to put the plug of the toaster into the side of the machine. I find that it is typical of a boy approaching teenage that he wishes to be by himself at times and I wonder whether he is also copying his brother. Again at church, he indicated by wriggling fiercely that he didn't think he should continue to sit in his buggy. We then arranged a table and chair at the back where he could look at the big catalogues provided by a couple of ladies in the congregation. Recently he has sat up beside us, but the seat he would dearly like is the one beside the organist, Viv. One Sunday, on the way back from Communion, to everyone's amusement, he eluded Andy's grasp and went to sit by Viv. We now keep a firm hold on him as we walk by. He is beginning to kneel beautifully at the altar rail, and we are starting to think about the possibility of him being confirmed in due course.

In some respects, Peter operates at the level of a small child, but in others he seems much older. When Peter was a baby, we were told the old-fashioned theory that children with Down's Syndrome reach a plateau in their development at the age of seven. We have found this to be totally untrue. Peter makes slow progress and provides us with challenge at all stages. We now begin to wonder more seriously what the future will hold for him. Will he be able to go on a course for young people with special needs at a College of Further Education when he is sixteen? Shall we want him to live more independently when he is adult? How well would we cope with the wrench of allowing him to join a local group home or a home run by one of the voluntary organisations like Care or the Home Farm Trust? Would we get funding for the latter at a time of financial stringency? We feel that the over-riding consideration should be to see him happily settled before we are too old to look after him. These are the questions and thoughts that worry and nag away at all parents with mentally handicapped children.

In the meantime, as we look back over the years we realise how much we have learned. We appreciate more fully the value of simple pleasures, stopping to listen to birds singing, sharing a meal. In getting to know Peter's friends, we have come across levels of caring and self-lessness we had not met before, and we have been struck by the spontaneity and openness of those of them who are labelled 'mentally handicapped'.

Peter has illuminated our faith and given meaning for us to the Sermon on the Mount where the vulnerable are seen as blessed. Peter, in the main, is a happy child, but he can get frustrated. Our life together has not always been easy, but we have been enriched by seeing the world through Peter's eyes.

AFTERWORD

People with mental handicap

Some questions for discussion and debate

The words and phrases we use to describe people indicate our underlying attitude towards them. Careless talk in 'classifying' groups can cause hurt and pain. It is so easy, for example, to describe those with certain limitations as 'the mentally handicapped', yet that is, in effect, a wholly impersonal phrase. We should think of them as 'mentally handicapped *people*' or people with mental handicap.

It is also essential that we do not consider people with mental handicap as representative of some sort of percentage of normality, that is a percentage of ourselves. They are 'one hundred per cent people' in their own right, people 'made in the image of God'. It is as 100% people that they must be considered and accepted.

If these two important attitudes are seen as fundamental and necessary, then we can begin to look at the many questions that arise from mental handicap, in both realistic and constructive ways.

Here are some questions:

1. Do we value lives only for their financial productivity, so that one who contributes to, say, the Gross National Product is valued in proportion to his or her contribution, while one who is unable to contribute financially, to generate income, is valueless?

2. Should we help people with mental handicap to remain in their families? At any cost? At any *financial* cost?

(For example, will the Health Authority or the Department of Social Services meet all the costs incurred to help that person remain in their own home—not only home helps and incontinence pads, but education, mobility, respite care, etc?)

At any *familial* cost? No matter what the wear-and-tear on the family, the possible disruption, the stress and the strain, and the worry of 'What will happen after we die? Who will look after him or her then?'?

Should 'they', on the other hand, live in communities? They might be happier there. There might be better care, better provision. There might, alternatively, be maltreatment, deprivation, experimentation. Might a 'good Home' be better than a 'loving but inadequate home'? What level of care can we expect from loving but untrained families? From unloving and untrained families?

Does the young handicapped person have the right to grow up as his or her 'normal' brothers and sisters do, to achieve a measure of independence by living, with support, in an ordinary home within the community?

3. How do we justify the high caring ratio necessary for the physical and mental care of handicapped people? (What happens to their emotional and spiritual care?) All those carers could be working in hospitals, opening wards closed for lack of staff, looking after patients who will return to the community once they have been 'made better' to carry on their commercially-contributing lives.

4. What do mentally handicapped people contribute to the life of others? Do they provide an opportunity for

others to care, and to show that they care (the first 'care' being physical caring, the second an outward expression of loving)? Do they offer an opportunity to declare the value of each human being for what they are themselves, not for what they may give to, or provide for, others. They may create an opportunity for self-denying service, as in some convents where the whole life of the religious community revolves around the patients/guests/residents. But is this in fact doing less then justice to mentally handicapped people, making them a means rather than an end in themselves, people of value for their own sake?

5. Do people with a mental handicap, whether children or adults, suffer *mentally* because of their handicap? How much are they aware of it? Does the ridicule they may attract hurt them? Do they suffer emotionally from the deprivation of being mentally handicapped? Do they suffer spiritually? How does God feel about them? How do they think God feels about them? Are they of lesser or greater, or the same, value to Him as others around them? How do they feel about God? Do they feel anything about God?

6. Do the families suffer? Some will say that they do not, that they love their handicapped members, that they wouldn't change them for anything. They will say that their mentally handicapped daughter or son has brought new heights and depths of love and loving to the whole family. But is it more often the *parents* who are saying these things? What might others in the family feel? The youngster who cannot have swimming lessons because his handicapped brother needs swimming lessons and there is only enough money for one? Or the little sister who cannot go to Brownies because there is no-one to take her as her brother cannot be left

alone? Or older children who cannot go on school trips because their handicapped sibling absorbs all the available cash? The adolescents who are teased for having a 'fruit-cake' for a brother; who lose girl or boy-friend because those cannot cope with the existence or presence of a mentally handicapped member of the family? How can we—individually, as a local community, or as 'society'—help such families?

7. How much do the parents suffer from their blighted hopes, dashed expectations, diminished dreams? How do they suffer from the worry of who will care for their son or daughter when they themselves are unable to do so, or after they are dead? How many marriages break up with the stresses of caring for a mentally handi-capped child or adult?

What happens if, as part of their condition, the handi-capped person becomes very big and strong and cannot be controlled, whether at home or in public places? How much help can we, will we be willing to provide? Why are we providing it? To make ourselves feel good, benevolent, earning our reward? Because it is their right to require, demand of us all that we have to offer? What are they giving to us? What are we giving to them? Why is there a 'them/us' division at all?

People with mental handicap raise questions for us about giving and receiving. It is perhaps in the discovery of the right balance between these two concepts that progress in relationships lies. We must give to mentally handicapped *people* the right to life, the right to live (not simply to exist), the right to be accepted, respected and honoured both because they are "children of God" and because they are our equals—they are 100% people.

The gifts and talents, attributes and attitudes, that they offer must be gratefully received, and they themselves graciously received. 'Society' (and particularly goodwill bodies like the church) must allow them—no, provide them with—the opportunities to develop themselves to the full. They have the right to the best education they can absorb so that all they can offer is 'led out' ('*educare*') into the community.

It is no one's right to enact and enforce laws that compel families to bear burdens of suffering beyond their ability to endure. The balance in nurturing care between the home and 'the Home' is difficult to draw. In the end, families who can and want to look after a mentally handicapped member of the family must be free to do so and be wholly supported in their undertaking. The community must come to the aid of those who want to do it, but just cannot.

Denis Duncan

If readers feel they have constructive comment to make on the questions and issues raised by Through Peter's Eyes, *they are welcome to send them to the publisher, Arthur James Limited (One Cranbourne Road, London N10 2BT), who will pass them on to the author, the contributors or the Down's Syndrome Association.*

DOWN'S SYNDROME

Down's Syndrome is the largest single cause of mental handicap, affecting some one thousand babies born each year in the United Kingdom. Unlike many forms of handicap, the syndrome can be diagnosed before birth, but at that stage there is no means of knowing how affected a particular child will be.

The range of ability is very wide. At the top end, increasing numbers of children with Down's Syndrome achieve many skills; a number enter ordinary schools, including secondary level. At the other end of the scale, a small minority are profoundly handicapped.

Down's Syndrome is not a disease, but arises from a genetic accident (it can happen to any parents) at the time of conception. In the commonest form of Down's Syndrome, standard Trisomy 21, each cell in the body has an extra chromosome making 47 instead of 46. The chromosomal error which causes Down's Syndrome was not discovered until 1959 when it was confirmed by French scientist Professor Lejeune. The extra chromosome means that children and adults with Down's Syndrome share certain physical characteristics. Not every child with Down's Syndrome shares every characteristic, but it is often possible to recognise the condition in the first few days of life.

The most common signs are a smaller, rounder face, extra fold (epicanthal) over the eyelids, floppy muscles and looser joints. Children with Down's Syndrome tend to be shorter than their peers and have a tendency to weight-gain. Babies with Down's Syndrome have a higher proportion of heart problems and chest and sinus infections as well, but advances in medical knowledge and care have meant that adults with Down's Syndrome can live well into their fifties and beyond.

The Genetic Background

Standard Trisomy 21

About 96% of all children with Down's Syndrome fall into the Standard Trisomy 21 group. The parents have normal chromosomes, but the baby has three rather than the correct two chromosomes on pair No. 21. Standard Trisomy is also called Trisomy 21 or Trisomy G, because No. 21 is in the G group. It usually results from a 'mistake' in the division of the egg or sperm cell.

Translocation

Translocation is observed in about 3% of babies with Down's Syndrome and can take several forms. First, No. 21 chromosome becomes attached to another chromosome after an initial small break at the tip. In about half the people who have Translocation Down's Syndrome, the Translocation is a unique and sporadic occurrence and does not imply a high risk for recurrence in future pregnancies. In the other half, however, it happens because one or other parent, though having a normal balanced chromosomal make-up, happens to have one of the No. 21's translocated, or 'stuck-on' to another chromosome. In the latter situation, the risk of recurrence of Down's Syndrome for the parent concerned, or for other members of the family with the same translocation can be quite high.

Only chromosome studies can indicate who is at risk, and what size that risk is. This is established by a blood test. Either parent can carry a translocation without showing any symptoms, because he or she still carried the correct amount of genetic material, although some of it is out of place (translocated). The non-handicapped child received only one chromosome of pair 21 from each parent. But a parent with Translocation can pass on his or her normal chromosome 21 plus the out-of-place (translocated) chromosome 21. This gives the child too much chromosome 21 material.

Mosaicism

This is rare and accounts for about 2—3% of children with Down's Syndrome. As its name suggests, the distribution of trisomic cells is patchy, with different chromosome counts—46 in some and 47 in others. Mosaicism arises when some of the cells in an early developing baby divide abnormally. Being a mixture of normal and Down's cells, such a baby may show only partial features of the condition. Some of these babies fare better and look less affected than other babies with Down's Syndrome.

These notes on Down's Syndrome have been provided by The Down's Syndrome Association, 12-13 Clapham Common, Southside, London, SW4 7AA (01-720-0008)